The Films Of

Bing Crosby

By Robert Bookbinder

The Citadel Press   Secaucus, New Jersey

FOR MY MOTHER AND FATHER
Sunday, Monday and Always

ACKNOWLEDGMENTS

Paramount Pictures; Metro-Goldwyn-Mayer;
20th Century-Fox; Columbia Pictures; Melnor
Films, Ltd.; United Artists; Universal
Pictures; Warner Bros. Pictures. I would also
like to express my special thanks to the
following individuals and organizations for
help in gathering the stills, for contributing
important information or for providing
helpful advice: Phil Luboviski of The Larry
Edmunds Bookstore; Paula Klaw of Movie
Star News; Mark Ricci of The Memory Shop;
Rico and Dave Dore; Jeff Wildman; Robert
Cauterucio; Lee Collins; Russell Freedman,
Lester Glassner, Christopher Young, Neal
Peters, Eric Benson; Arlene Ludwig of Walt
Disney Productions and above all to both
Morris Greenblat and my friend and mentor
Louis Freedman for their much appreciated
help and guidance.

Second printing
Copyright 1977 by Robert Bookbinder
All rights reserved
Published by Citadel Press
A division of Lyle Stuart Inc.
120 Enterprise Ave., Secaucus, N. J. 07094
In Canada: George J. McLeod Limited, Toronto
Manufactured in the United States of America by
Halliday Lithograph Corp., West Hanover, Mass.
DESIGNED BY LESTER GLASSNER

Library of Congress Cataloging in Publication Data
Bookbinder, Robert.
The films of Bing Crosby.
1. Crosby, Bing, 1904- I. Title.
ML420.C939B6   790.2'092'4   77-23975
ISBN 0-8065-0598-2

Contents

Maurice Seymour

BING CROSBY: INTRODUCTION TO A LEGEND

At one time, Bing Crosby was the most popular screen star in the history of motion pictures. He completely dominated the motion-picture box offices across the country for almost ten years, and he has had more box-office hits than any other screen performer. This is a phenomenon when one considers that Bing Crosby was the complete opposite of such sturdy screen stars as Clark Gable, Errol Flynn, Humphrey Bogart, James Cagney, and Gary Cooper. Unlike any of them, Crosby was never thought of as being exclusively a film star, because he was not a larger-than-life personality. On screen, Crosby did nothing more than exude an aura of friendliness and easy-going charm that the movie-going public came to regard as a welcome change of pace from the often contrived screen images of some other stars. He emerged as the public's favorite film attraction between 1944 and 1949.

It is easy to understand why Bing Crosby rose to success as a singer and recording star. His pleasant, modulated baritone easily lent itself to a wide variety of vocal acrobatics, and it was deep enough and appealing enough to touch even the hardest of female hearts. But it must be remembered that not every singer, regardless of how unique his voice, can attain the same measure of success in front of a motion-picture camera. A number of the most popular singers, such as Al Jolson and Rudy Vallee, failed to register on the screen because they did not possess that peculiar and often baffling commercial commodity known as "movie-star quality."

Bing Crosby, however, was a popular singer with a liberal dose of this quality, and therefore, he was tremendously successful in making the transition from records and radio to the films. Of course, the transition was hardly an easy one, even for Bing Crosby. His first three or four performances are burdened with an awkwardness that makes it plain to almost any audience that the young "crooner turned movie star" was exceedingly self-conscious in

Paul Whiteman's "Rhythm Boys"

front of a camera. He had not yet mastered the difficulty art of reacting to his fellow performers instead of exclusively to the camera. However, Crosby soon conquered his difficulties; before long he was able to establish himself as a light-comedic leading man of considerable personality and skill.

During most of the 1930s, Crosby's screen roles were all essentially of the same type of character. He was invariably cast as a romanticized version of himself, almost always in the role of an easy-going crooner who falls in love with a beauteous young lady and spends the greater portion of his screen time melting her heart with the nicest and most popular love songs of the period.

Seen today, most of the Crosby films produced during the 1930s don't hold up very well. Their only real cinematic merit is that Crosby is the star. If any of them have any kind of immortality, it is entirely due to Crosby's presence and the lasting quality of the songs Bing sang.

But if the Crosby films produced during his first ten years in Hollywood leave a great deal to be desired, there is no denying that his films produced between 1939 and 1949 are among the most enjoyable pictures of their kind. Unpretentious and loaded with entertainment value, Crosby's Paramount musicals of the 1940s are almost all top quality, as well as being some of the best-remembered joys of the screen during that decade. In films like *Rhythm on the River, Birth of the Blues, Holiday Inn, Dixie, Going My Way, Here Come the Waves, Bells of St. Mary's, Blue Skies, The Emperor Waltz, A Connecticut Yankee in King Arthur's Court*, and, of course, the forever popular *Road* pictures with the Bingle's friendliest "enemy," Bob Hope, both Crosby and his studio reached a seldom-equaled level of proficiency in musical cinema.

It wasn't really the grand, opulent sort of excellence that Metro-Goldwyn-Mayer brought to most of their musical outings during the forties and fifties, nor was it the wonderfully "campy" quality that 20th Century-Fox invariably lavished on its Betty Grable–John Payne films. Instead, Paramount and Crosby wisely concentrated on creating an unmistakable atmosphere and mood, enabling the audience to become totally involved in what was going on.

This "mood" was achieved not only through carefully casting Crosby against performers who complemented his screen image (such as Hope, Astaire, Lamour, Barry Fitzgerald, Joan Caulfield, and Marjorie Reynolds), but also through the skillful use of scenic design, costuming, musical scoring, and photography. The correct combination of all these elements, coupled with Crosby's screen personality and the songs of such composers as Irving Berlin, Harold Arlen, James Van Heusen, and Johnny Burke, made Bing's forties musicals truly creative films.

Bing was born Harry Lillis Crosby, Jr., on May 2, 1904. Although he was born in Tacoma, Washington, young Bing spent most of his childhood and early adult life in Spokane (hence the popular nickname "The Kid from Spokane"). Bing revealed in his autobiography that his mother, Catherine Harrigan Crosby, and his father, Harry Crosby, Sr., came from a long and distinguished line of pioneering settlers and that Crosby, Sr., an easygoing and very wonderful man, worked as the accountant for a beer manufacturer.

As a boy growing up in the rough-and-tumble atmosphere of industrial Spokane, Bing became proficient at a wide variety of sports, including baseball and football, and he frequently found it necessary to brush up on his boxing when one of the neighborhood hellions made himself obnoxious. (Perhaps his early interest and ability at these sports accounts for his later passion for golf, hunting and fishing).

Like most of the other children in Spokane, Crosby attended elementary school at Webster

School and became a student at Gonzaga High School from 1917 to 1921. Not really possessing a burning interest in academic pursuits, the enterprising young Bing channeled his energies into the pursuit of extra money by working as a ranch hand, a lumberjack, a janitor, and a newspaper carrier. But none of these jobs appealed to young Crosby as much as the idea of entering music and entertainment on a professional basis.

Crosby's penchant for music and singing stemmed back to his early childhood. Crosby has often attributed his intense love of music to the home life he led as a youngster. Both Bing's parents were musically inclined, and the Crosby home was a place in which devotion to music was nothing less than gospel. In fact, Pop Crosby made certain that every one of his children would grow up with an understanding, respect, and love of music, and he often made financial sacrifices to purchase a musical instrument from which he felt his children could benefit. As a fortunate result, Bing grew up in a kind of musical world and was therefore prepared for the later years when he often found it necessary to "sing for his supper."

Upon his graduation from high school, Bing went on to Gonzaga University, where his urge to perform professionally really began to intensify. Because of this, Crosby and his piano-playing boyhood chum Al Rinker decided to devote much of their spare time to their mutual love of music, and before long they began playing local engagements with a small instrumental ensemble. In the meantime, Crosby decided to study law at Gonzaga University, but even this did nothing to squelch his overwhelming desire for a life in front of the footlights.

Not surprisingly, Crosby and Rinker decided to team as a vocal-instrumental duo (Rinker on piano, Crosby playing the drums and singing). They also concluded that they were skillful enough and unique enough to take the big city of Los Angeles by storm. Crosby subsequently forsook his legal studies, and he and Rinker ventured to Los Angeles in the hope of finding a job in entertainment.

Once the boys arrived in Los Angeles, they didn't exactly take the city by storm, but they did secure an engagement at a local theater, the Boulevard. Following this, Crosby and Rinker did a series of successful stints in and around Los Angeles and quickly began to establish a reputation.

In 1927, word of their skill reached the ears of the most important orchestra leader of the day, Paul Whiteman. Deciding to give Bing and Al a much-deserved break, Whiteman quickly signed them up to do service with his orchestra. Through their association with Whiteman, Crosby and Rinker met another young performer named Harry Barris. As a result of this fateful meeting, Whiteman decided to use Crosby, Barris, and Rinker as a vocal-instrumental trio, an "added attraction" with the Whiteman band. The talented threesome was named the Rhythm Boys trio. The trio would one day emerge as a minor legend in the history of show business, not only because Crosby's association with the small group was his first real step up the ladder, but also because the trio was well-known for continually exasperating Whiteman with their often uncontrolled ad-libbing and fooling around during supposedly serious performances.

The team's nutty antics, coupled with the fact that Crosby, Barris, and Rinker would often disappear for days at a time without leaving word where they would be, served as a constant strain on their relationship with the Whiteman troupe. After appearing briefly with Whiteman and his band in the lavish motion picture *King of Jazz* in 1930, the Rhythm Boys left the Whiteman orchestra to try their luck elsewhere. The group was quickly snatched up by another enterprising bandleader, Gus Arnheim, and began to achieve a certain de-

With wife Dixie Lee and baby Gary

13

gree of notoriety over the radio and on records, but the Rhythm Boys ultimately disbanded in 1931.

During 1930, two significant events took place in Bing's life. The first was his marriage to a beautiful young woman named Wilma Winfred Wyatt (motion-picture actress Dixie Lee), who, at the time of their marriage, was actually more of a celebrity than Bing. She had appeared in several motion pictures for the Fox Film Corporation, including *Fox Movietone Follies of 1929, Happy Days, Why Leave Home?, Let's Go Places,* and *No Limit.* After her marriage to Bing, however, Dixie Lee appeared in only one more film (the title of which, ironically, was taken from one of Bing's hit songs, "Love in Bloom").

The second important event was that at this time Bing got his first real taste of the cinema, appearing as the star of a string of two-reel comedies, most produced by Mack Sennett. Although Bing had little to do in these shorts except cavort comically and sing, they still provided him with valuable training in front of a camera.

One frequently hears about the phenomenon known as "overnight stardom," but the term was perhaps never more accurate than in describing Bing Crosby's skyrocketing trip to fame and recognition. One year after his marriage to Dixie Lee, Bing was thrust into almost instantaneous nationwide popularity through a series of starring radio appearances and a long and successful run on stage at New York's Paramount Theatre. A gigantic billboard erected in New York City advertised Crosby's appearance, billing him as "The Romantic Singer of Songs You Love."

Glancing over virtually every Crosby interview over the past quarter century, one always gets the impression that Crosby would probably have been content to spend the rest of his professional life playing small nightclub engagements with Rinker and Barris and that he views his almost unequaled success as the result of a long series of lucky accidents. In fact, all the way through his autobiography, *Call Me Lucky* (published in 1953), Crosby continually emphasizes that he has been fortunate all his life. Like most other performers who have reached the pinnacle of show-business success, Crosby retains an aura of complete modesty.

Perhaps this air of modesty helped make Crosby such a totally appealing and likable film personality. In almost every one of his more than sixty-five motion pictures (including twenty "cameo" appearances), Bing Crosby never failed to give the refreshing impression that he was nothing more than an ordinary guy having a lot of fun up there on the screen. Unlike many other major screen stars, Crosby had no pretensions about himself or his work. He realized that his abilities as an actor were limited and that a star's success is often short-lived. But Crosby never realized that he often executed a truly memorable screen performance, no matter how shallow and one-dimensional his role.

Not only did Crosby possess a natural acting ability, but he frequently made the most of a screen role of limited dimension and depth. In lightly written musicals like *Birth of the Blues, Dixie, Holiday Inn, Blue Skies*, and *The Emperor Waltz*, Crosby transcended the limitations of his material and turned in performances of surprising scope and substance.

Further, although Bing was just playing himself in about 90 percent of his films, he nevertheless gave nearly every one of his screen characters a distinct personality all its own.

For example, the characters of Joe Beebe in *Sing You Sinners* and Johnny Adams in *Blue Skies* are fundamentally the same—they are both fun-loving, irresponsible, and impossible for anyone to dislike. But as a result of his often unacknowledged skill as a straight actor, Crosby was able to give them contrasting personality characteristics that

With the Boswell Sisters, c. 1932

made Joe Beebe and Johnny Adams similar on the surface, yet very different in their reactions to the world around them. Joe Beebe appears in *Sing You Sinners* as a fun-loving character who often questions his own irresponsible behavior but also seems incapable of mending his ways, no matter how much his conduct hurts his mother (Elizabeth Patterson) and his two brothers (Fred MacMurray and Donald O'Connor). However, Johnny Adams, in *Blue Skies*, is something else again. He does possess the same kind of "live for the moment" philosophy, but he emerges as much more compassionate, because he finally grows into a responsible adult after he discovers how his inability to settle down contributed to the breakup of his once-happy marriage (to Joan Caulfield). Whether playing a challenging dramatic role like that of Frank Elgin in *The Country Girl* or simply tackling a relatively easy assignment like the part of songwriter Dan Emmett in the film *Dixie,* Crosby invariably brought a compelling sensitivity to his roles that made each of them endearing despite the personal faults of the characters.

In most of his films of the late thirties and the forties, Crosby also brought this sensitivity to his interpretations of the songs he sang, often making these songs into unforgettable moments that enhanced the films' effectiveness. Crosby was also capable of giving a wide variety of vocal interpretations to his songs and he could effortlessly render a torch song (such as "Temptation" in *Going Hollywood*), a bouncy incidental number (like "Ain't Got a Dime to My Name" in *Road to Morocco* and "It's Anybody's Spring" in *Road to Utopia*), or a sentimental love song (such as "But Beautiful" in *Road to Rio* and "The Kiss in Your Eyes" in *The Emperor Waltz*) with equal skill and effectiveness.

The Bing Crosby image on screen was relatively simple, almost always that of an easy-living vaga-

With Gene Raymond and Charles Starrett

With wife Dixie Lee and sons Dennis and Phillip

bond who despises work and is more than content to live his life as a "free spirit." This image was successful not only because it was a reflection of what Bing was like in real life, but also because it is the kind of screen image with which movie audiences identify. Nothing could relax a battle-fatigued wartime audience more than stretching out in a movie theater for ninety carefree minutes to watch the easygoing Bingle casually thumb his nose at society's ludicrous stuffiness and warbling a collection of Burke–Van Heusen tunes that usually fit in beautifully with the Crosby charisma. Crosby's image as a happy-go-lucky roustabout, coupled with the fact that Bing reminded people of "the guy next door," allowed frustrated filmgoers to see a bit of themselves in Crosby.

Not surprisingly, almost every one of Bing's motion pictures during this period was among the top-grossing films of the year.

Bing Crosby's film career can be divided into three distinct phases. The first lasted from 1932 to 1938. During this time Crosby's films always featured him as a boyish crooner who didn't take much of anything seriously and was almost always capable of breaking down a beautiful young lady's defenses by crooning "May I?" or "Sweet Leilani." Almost every Crosby film during this period lacked a tangible plotline; their emphasis was on Crosby's undeniable ability as a singer of light, romantic tunes. Not surprisingly, the songs emerged as the real stars of these films, more than compensating for the ridiculous and often nonexistent plotlines.

As Crosby's film career progressed into the late thirties and early forties, however, Bing moved into the most memorable and productive stage of his career. During this time, Paramount Pictures really allowed Bing to come into his own by increasing the budgets and improving the storylines.

The third stage began in 1950 and continues now. During this era, Bing branched out into straight dramatic acting in four truly memorable films. He proved that he was capable of carrying a motion picture without singing. However, most of his musicals and light comedies during this period were drastically inferior to his forties' efforts, and almost all of them emerged as merely average screen exercises, unworthy of Bing's talents. This is disappointing, but during the fifties most great film stars of the thirties and forties were reduced to performing in unworthy vehicles. With very few exceptions, like Humphrey Bogart and Gary Cooper, they almost all found themselves in fewer films.

Crosby's astounding success at the Paramount Theatre in New York and the fame he was gaining from his radio appearances motivated Paramount Pictures (then known as Paramount Publix) to place the young crooner under contract as a possible candidate for film stardom. Crosby's initial appearance as a motion picture star was in *The Big Broadcast*, which explored the medium that had made Crosby such a success—radio. Released in 1932, the film contained many diverse moments of comedy and song. It was a well-produced showcase wherein such sparkling personalities as Kate Smith, the Mills Brothers, the Boswell Sisters, Cab Calloway, George Burns, Gracie Allen, and Stuart Erwin performed in a manner not unlike what they had been doing on radio for many years. The film was nicely directed by Frank Tuttle (who directed many of Crosby's best films during the subsequent eight years) and featured fairly astute (for the period) photography by George Folsey. However, *The Big Broadcast* was considered too unorthodox at the time, and although audiences loved it, it received mixed reviews from most of the important critics. The film has, however, become a minor classic with the passage of time; it is a particular favorite among film buffs and students interested in Hollywood's earliest efforts at musical revues.

With Jack Oakie and Toby Wing

Billboard of Crosby at the Paramount Theatre shortly before his movie fame

General
EVERY
WEEK
AT THE CROSS ROADS
OF THE WORLD!
Param
RADIO'S
BING
Romantic singer
BUILDER E.E.HIRTLE BUILDER
CARPENTER

Between scenes of Pennies From Heaven *with Dixie Lee and co-star Edith Fellows*

Crosby's second starring vehicle was even better. A humorous, often hilarious musical glimpse at the goofy goings-on at a small Midwestern university, *College Humor* admittedly didn't contain much of a story but did offer several highly amusing interludes featuring Jack Oakie, George Burns, and Gracie Allen, as well as a couple of memorable songs sung by Crosby, including the popular "Learn to Croon."

College Humor and Crosby's third picture, *Too Much Harmony*, both received some excellent critical reviews as well as some bad ones. The main topic of most of these notices was, of course, Crosby. Most critics found him a strong contender for stardom; however, some reviewers were less than impressed with his as yet undiscovered abilities as an actor. Most of these critics commented that Crosby could not yet sustain a believable characterization. This is basically true; however, there is no denying that Crosby's roles in these films were very weakly written and understandably difficult for him to make believable. As a result, his acting in these early films is distinctly limited, lacking the style and credibility he brought to most of his later characterizations. Nearly all the critics did agree that Bing's singing voice was one of the most original and pleasant sounds ever to emerge from a motion picture.

1933's *Going Hollywood* teamed Crosby with Marion Davies. It was one of the few Crosby films produced between 1932 and 1956 that was not a product of Paramount Pictures. Produced by William Randolph Hearst's Cosmopolitan Productions, in conjunction with Metro-Goldwyn-Mayer, *Going Hollywood* also featured nice supporting performances from Fifi D'Orsay, Stuart Erwin, and Ned Sparks. Because it was one of those "behind-the-scenes" formula pictures that movie audiences of the thirties loved so well, *Going Hollywood* was a great box-office success.

Crosby's next three screen vehicles were all based

upon works originally presented on the stage. The first and by far the best of these was a little musical comedy entitled *We're Not Dressing*. Based upon a play by Sir James Barrie entitled *The Admirable Crichton*, the film did much to establish Bing Crosby's likable image as an ordinary guy who falls deeply in love with a beautiful, high-class woman (Carole Lombard) but convinces himself that his meager station in life would make it impossible for her to love him. Of course, Bing ultimately wins Carole's heart.

With this film, Bing proved that his skills as a screen performer were beginning to improve. This, coupled with Bing's support by George Burns, Gracie Allen, Ethel Merman, and a young Ray Milland in one of his earliest film appearances, made *We're Not Dressing* one of Bing's best films of the 1930s.

Crosby's most elaborate and costly motion picture during this period was A. Edward Sutherland's *Mississippi*. Aside from a dazzling visual production and a great performance by W. C. Fields as a comical riverboat skipper, *Mississippi* featured two excellent vocal interpretations by Crosby, "Easy to Remember" and "Down by the River." Further contributing to the film's box office success, Paramount wisely invested *Mississippi* with a high budget, beautiful scenic designs, and tasteful cinematography.

By 1935, Bing's continued success as a screen star was insured, but Crosby still remembered that only six years before he had been simply one of the Rhythm Boys. That group dissolved in 1931, but Crosby remained good friends with both Al Rinker and Harry Barris. Later on, when Crosby really hit his stride as a superstar, Harry Barris often appeared briefly in Crosby's films as a bandleader or a jive-happy, gum-chewing little jazzman. As a result, Barris became a familiar face in the Paramount stock company, and he also appeared in several non-Crosby films. Probably Barris's most famous ap-

With prize 145-pound marlin

With Brother Bob Crosby

At the races with wife Dixie Lee

pearance was in *The Lost Weekend* as the sarcastic piano player who taunts accused purse snatcher Ray Milland by singing a derisive parody of "Somebody Stole My Gal," substituting "stole the purse" for the proper lyrics.

Crosby's last picture of 1935 was an inconsequential little item, *Two For Tonight*. By the same token, 1936's *Anything Goes* was nothing to write home about. It contained only one memorable sequence, wherein a bearded Bing Crosby sang a spirited duet of Cole Porter's "You're the Top" with co-star Ethel Merman.

Rhythm on the Range was much, much better. A clever musical Western that featured Crosby as a rough-and-tumble cowboy, the film is remembered today as the springboard for Martha Raye's film career. However, *Rhythm on the Range* is also noteworthy among Crosby's musicals of the thirties because it contained an intelligent plotline that never got lost. In addition, the film allowed Crosby to wrap his mellow tones around some flavorful Western songs. Crosby delivered them all with equal finesse, but the highlight surely had to be Bing's beautiful, almost haunting rendition of Billy Hill's superb tribute to the old West, "Empty Saddles," a thoughtful and often moving ballad that fit Crosby's smooth voice like a tailor-made glove. Bing's dramatic, echoing interpretation, sung from the middle of a rodeo stadium, gives it an unreal, almost ghostly quality.

In 1936, Paramount loaned Crosby to Columbia Pictures to star in *Pennies from Heaven*. Crosby's trip to Columbia was hardly worth the trouble. *Pennies from Heaven* emerged as a dull and sometimes incongruous film. Despite some first-rate vocalizing by Crosby, especially in the title tune, and a brief but amusing tongue-in-cheek interlude in which Louis Armstrong sang a gag song called "Skeleton in the Closet," *Pennies from Heaven* hasn't held up over the years. Surprisingly, the picture was highly praised by most critics. Perhaps the audiences of 1936 found the picture's corn and blatant sentiment charming.

Since Bing Crosby's annual earnings through records, radio, and motion pictures were nearly a quarter of a million dollars, in 1935 Bing and his business advisor (his older brother Everett Crosby) wisely decided to form a corporation. The name of the corporation was "Bing Crosby, Ltd., Incorporated," and its board of directors was composed of Bing, Everett, their brother Larry, and their father, Harry Crosby, Sr. The building that housed the corporation was on the Paramount lot, so Bing could conduct the corporation's business while taking time out from his duties in motion pictures.

With the enormous success of *Rhythm on the Range*, one of the top grossers of 1936, Paramount reteamed Bing Crosby with Martha Raye in two highly successful comedies, *Waikiki Wedding* and *Double or Nothing*, both produced in 1937. The first picture was a Hawaiian frolic that also cast Crosby opposite Shirley Ross, who became his most consistently popular leading lady during the 1930s. It was directed by Frank Tuttle and contained a number of impressive supporting performances from Bob "Bazooka" Burns, George Barbier, and Leif Erickson. The second film, *Double or Nothing,* was not as good but still emerged as an entertaining little opus in which Crosby sang "The Moon Got in My Eyes."

Even the worst of the Crosby films of the 1930s is still mildly enjoyable because of the songs and because of Bing's personality. But Crosby's next film for Paramount, *Doctor Rhythm*, had no redeeming values, except Beatrice Lillie's brief but hilarious appearances. Bing's next film, however, was the best in which he appeared during the thirties. With a warm and touching story by Claude Binyon and co-stars the caliber of Fred MacMurray, Elizabeth Patterson, and Donald O'Connor (making his mo-

Attending tennis tourney with Edmund Lowe, Donald Budge and Rubye De Remer

tion picture debut), *Sing You Sinners* could hardly miss success.

Aside from Crosby's excellent performance as the happy-go-lucky protagonist, Joe Beebe, perhaps the most memorable sequence in *Sing You Sinners* was the famous "Small Fry" musical number in which Crosby appeared as a bespectacled old seafarer and MacMurray appeared as Bing's oversized wife. The song's title refers to the mismatched couple's nasty little son (O'Connor), and during the song Crosby chastises the lad for his evil ways while "Mother MacMurray" knits frantically and puffs an unlit corncob pipe and occasionally agrees with Crosby's accusations by nodding and repeating, "Oh, yes! Oh, yes! Oh, yes!" with a delightful air of mock disapproval. Beautifully absurd and often hilarious, the "Small Fry" routine remains a golden moment of cinematic comedy, one of the most impressive sequences ever to grace a Bing Crosby film.

The success of "the Groaner" in a sturdy screen vehicle like *Sing You Sinners* perhaps prompted the studio to steer Crosby's film career on a new, very different course. Immediately following *Sing You Sinners,* Crosby's vehicles at Paramount began to improve drastically in production, scripting, and direction. As a result, Crosby begain to attain new importance and prestige as a film personality.

After performing in *Paris Honeymoon*, a pleasantly hectic comedy at Paramount, Crosby was loaned to Universal Pictures for an enjoyable sentimental farce called *East Side of Heaven*. Like *Sing You Sinners* and *Rhythm on the Range,* this film contained a plausible plotline, and it was blessed with a distinguished supporting cast including Joan Blondell, Mischa Auer, Sir C. Aubrey Smith, and Irene Hervey.

On October 21, 1937, Bing Crosby's alma mater Gonzaga University, surprised the performer by conferring upon him the degree of doctor of philosophy in music. The event was, of course, well-covered by the press, and Crosby later revealed that although he appreciated the gesture, he found it extremely difficult to take seriously. A large portion of the academic community shared Bing's sentiments, but still, such an honor wasn't bad for a college dropout.

Returning to his home studio after completing *East Side of Heaven*, Crosby starred in *The Star Maker*, a ludicrous film supposedly based on the life of Gus Edwards. Its only real merits were musical numbers performed by a large group of children and a clever sequence wherein the audience was invited to sing along with Crosby and Irene Ware in a spirited rendition of "School Days."

Next came the most important motion picture in the film careers of both Bing Crosby and Bob Hope. A modestly produced and occasionally amusing little picture, *The Road to Singapore* was, of course, the beginning of perhaps the most successful movie series in the history of motion pictures, the *Road* series. The six original *Road* adventures were all produced by Paramount Pictures between 1940 and 1952. Almost all of them contained the same basic plotline, with Hope and Crosby as the perennial pair of happy-go-lucky song-and-dance men who get involved in cliff-hanging adventures during visits to such faraway locales as Singapore, Zanzibar, Morocco, Utopia (Alaska), Rio, and Bali.

The plot formula in a *Road* film was of little importance, merely serving as an excuse for the comedy patter of Hope and Crosby. All of the films were successful, and every one was among the biggest moneymakers during the year of its release.

There are many reasons for the series' enormous success, but perhaps the most important was that the *Road* films were examples of Hollywood at its absolute wildest. Paramount Pictures must have been a film studio with a tremendous sense of humor—the studio repeatedly poked fun at itself in these films. (In *Road to Utopia,* Bob and Bing come

On the Paramount lot during the filming of Variety Girl.

across a snow-capped Alaskan mountain peak. Bob suddenly says, "Look at all that bread and butter!" Bing, of course, hasn't the vaguest idea what Hope is talking about. He asks, "What do you mean bread and butter. That's nothing but a mountain." At this point, the mountain is magically transformed into the Paramount Pictures trademark, and Bob remarks, "It may be just a mountain to you, but it's bread and butter to me!").

Paramount also allowed Hope and Crosby to perform in a manner that had rarely been witnessed on the screen. Prior to the *Road* series, it would have been unthinkable for a studio to let actors disregard the script and just "wing it." But the shrewd studio knew exactly what it was doing. Perhaps Paramount realized that Bob and Bing were possibly the only two comics in Hollywood who could get away with such ridiculous antics and that to stifle their creativity would only have jeopardized the success of the series. Indeed, the most enjoyable thing about the *Road* pictures is that Hope and Crosby *are* playing it by ear and having one great time in the process.

All things considered, perhaps the line that best sums up the satirical spirit of the *Road* adventures is a verse from "We're Off on the Road to Morocco" (written by James Van Heusen and Johnny Burke), which Bing and Bob sang perched atop a camel in *Road to Morocco*. Riding casually amid the sand dunes of the Sahara, Bing and Bob tell the audience, in song, that they are about to embark on another dangerous adventure in an exotic locale and anticipate running into life-threatening situations. However, about halfway through the song, the boys assure their followers that they are in no real danger: "For any villains we may meet we haven't any fears. Paramount will protect us 'cause we're signed for five more years."

After a starring appearance at Universal in *If I Had My Way*, Crosby undertook the lead in his last and best film of 1940, *Rhythm on the River*. This film proved that Paramount was beginning to produce their Bing Crosby vehicles with greater care. A superbly constructed comedy starring Crosby, Mary Martin, and Basil Rathbone, *Rhythm on the River* was an excellent picture in which both Bing and Mary had many opportunities to show off their superb singing. Martin was outstanding in her delivery of a jaunty little song called "Ain't It a Shame about Mame," in which she was accompanied by Bing's good buddy Harry Barris, seen standing behind her blowing out a jazzy backup on a hot saxophone. "Only Forever," one of the songs James Monaco and Johnny Burke composed for *Rhythm on the River*, was nominated for a Best Song Oscar in 1940.

1941 found Crosby starring opposite Mary Martin in a motion picture about jazz entitled *Birth of the Blues* and opposite Bob Hope in *Road to Zanzibar*, the second film in the *Road* series. Both were enjoyable films that received favorable reviews from nearly all the important critics, most of whom remarked that *Road to Zanzibar* was an improvement over the first film of the series.

Zanzibar's success established Crosby and Hope as the moviegoing public's favorite comedy team. As a result, they both found the popularity of their solo vehicles increasing. Both performers also continued to make starring appearances together on radio, frequently cavorting in a manner similar to their antics in the *Road* films, and Hope and Crosby quickly became the hottest twosome in show business. (It could be argued that during this period Bud Abbott and Lou Costello were the kings of comedy, but only one of their pictures, *Abbott and Costello Meet Frankenstein*, was ever among the

With Bob Hope

With Frank Sinatra

biggest moneymakers of the year. Virtually every one of Hope and Crosby's team efforts and solo vehicles was a box-office blockbuster.

The pair's phenomenal film success came about mainly because both performers were in the right place at the right time with the right sort of talent. The onset of the Second World War intensified the filmgoing public's appetite for "escapist" entertainment, at which Crosby and Hope were most adept. As a result, audiences welcomed the goofy nonsense of the *Road* series with open arms.

Crosby's films of the 1940s were all typical Paramount productions, and each bore the unmistakable trademarks of that studio. Like Bob Hope's "straight" comedy vehicles, Crosby's musical comedies almost all contained an element of goofiness (which may have been less sophisticated than the "high-class" farces of other studios but was infinitely more enjoyable), always enhanced by flawless production. Realizing that Metro, Warners, and Universal had the undisputed corners on literary adaptations, contemporary dramas, and horror films, respectively, Paramount wisely avoided these areas and went on to lead the industry in comedies, musicals, and melodramas, starring such sturdy box-office names as Crosby, Hope, Ray Milland, Fred MacMurray, Alan Ladd, Dorothy Lamour, Paulette Goddard, Veronica Lake, Betty Hutton, Robert Preston, and Eddie Bracken.

If Paramount could have looked into the future in 1942, they might have been surprised to discover that they would one day feature their star crooner as the lead in a couple of heavy, no-nonsense, and virtually songless dramas, *Little Boy Lost* and *The Country Girl*. The studio would have also been surprised to learn that the easy-going "Groaner" would also be in hot competition with Marlon Brando for the Best Actor Oscar of 1954. But in 1942 Paramount had no crystal balls on the lot (except, of course, the kind used in movies) and was content to continue starring Crosby in the light-hearted musical vehicles for which he had become so famous and well loved.

For all the success of the *Road* films and in spite of the magic that sparked every time Hope and Crosby got together, perhaps the most memorable teaming of Crosby's screen career occurred when Paramount dreamed up the notion of bringing the undisputed monarchs of the musical cinema together in a screenplay also featuring an impressive collection of songs by Irving Berlin. As if bringing Crosby, Astaire, and Berlin together wasn't enough to boggle the mind, Paramount assigned its direction to Mark Sandrich, the man responsible for most of the best of the Fred Astaire–Ginger Rogers musicals of the thirties. The Crosby-Astaire-Berlin-Sandrich collaboration reached the theaters as *Holiday Inn*. This was the film in which he introduced the song that would one day emerge not only as Crosby's greatest single record hit, but also as the largest-selling record of our time, "White Christmas."

Crosby next appeared with Hope in *Road to Morocco* and opposite virtually every other star under contract to Paramount in a spirited all-star musical spectacular, *Star Spangled Rhythm.* In the latter Crosby sang one song and appeared briefly as himself arriving for work on the Paramount lot with his young son Gary (born in 1933). The genial guard at the studio gate asks Gary if he has come to watch his dad make pictures, but the lad tells him, "Nah. Dorothy Lamour's workin' today." Crosby puts his arm around Gary and explains that the child "listens to Hope too much."

Although jokes of this nature may seem corny today, they illustrate the kind of lame nonsense that both Crosby and Hope could get away with during this period. The audiences of 1943 didn't regard these jokes as any funnier than a modern audience would, but they accepted them because they were

With Dinah Shore

an important part of the Hope and Crosby charm. The filmgoing public didn't care how bad the jokes were or how weak the storyline was; they were interested only in being entertained by the marvelous personalities of Bob and Bing.

Between pictures, Bing took part in a historic event at the National Broadcasting Company in Hollywood in early July 1943. The original Rhythm Boys, Crosby, Al Rinker, and Harry Barris, got together briefly with their old mentor Paul Whiteman and his orchestra and sang a few choruses of one of their most popular songs from the old days, Harry Barris's "Mississippi Mud."

Bing's wife, Dixie Lee, had given up her film career to devote herself to her home and family. Her marriage to Crosby had produced four sons, Gary, Dennis and Phillip (both born in 1934), and Lindsay (born in 1939).

All four boys tried their hand at performing, but only Gary, the eldest, had any success. He has appeared in a number of popular films (including *Mardi Gras*; *Holiday for Lovers*, an amusing comedy in which he supported Clifton Webb and his father's old co-star Jane Wyman; and Elvis Presley's *Girl Happy*) and a number of successful television series, most notably "Adam-12" and "Chase." He has proved an effective TV actor, capable of rising above inferior material in a manner not unlike his famous father. Because of this, Gary Crosby has often been largely responsible for the quality of the TV shows in which he appears.

Bing Crosby's first appearance before a Technicolor camera was as the famous American composer and minstrel entertainer Dan Emmett, in *Dixie*. Of course, this was not a very accurate biography, but it was a visually beautiful motion picture that featured some nicely staged minstrel numbers.

Although Crosby's first film of 1944 is listed as *Going My Way*, many film scholars speculate that the Crosby picture immediately following *Dixie* was actually *Road to Utopia*, made in early 1944 but for some reason not released until two years later. Although it would be difficult to prove that *Road to Utopia* was produced before *Going My Way*, several pieces of evidence in *Road to Utopia* lead almost any observant viewer to believe this. For instance, in the song "Put It There Pal" in *Road to Utopia*, Crosby and Hope refer to their last solo vehicles as *Dixie* and *Let's Face It*, both produced in 1943. Also, *Road to Utopia* features humorist Robert Benchley in the role of the film's comical "narrator," and since Benchley died in 1945 it would have been impossible for him to appear in a film in 1946.

One can only guess why Paramount would shelve a *Road* film for two years, but perhaps the studio thought the picture a little *too* zany, even for Hope and Crosby. *Road to Utopia* was the wackiest of all the *Road* pictures with more crazy jokes, talking animals, and senseless dialogue than all the others combined.

Paramount may have been apprehensive about unleashing such a wild film, but it emerged as one of the most successful and honored pictures of 1946. *Road to Utopia* received an Oscar nomination (for Best Screenplay, of all things), was praised by the hard-to-impress dean of movie critics Bosley Crowther, and was named one of the Ten Best Films of the year by *The New York Times*. As a result, *Road to Utopia* is looked upon as one of Hollywood's most remarkable flukes, one of its most inexplicable triumphs.

In mid-1944 producer-director Leo McCarey conceived of transferring his original story "Going My Way" to the motion-picture screen. A charming and sentimental tale about the relationship between an unorthodox young priest and a stodgy, tradition-bound older one, McCarey's story was unique among religious properties because it approached religion in a manner never before attempted on the

With Fred Astaire in France during a 1944 USO tour

With Bette Davis

Crosby displays spirit for his own team, the Pittsburgh Pirates

With John Scott Trotter and Ethel Merman

screen. It attempted to depict religion as a bright and rewarding human experience instead of some dark, forbidding mystery. This refreshing approach was exemplified by the story's easygoing protagonist, Father Chuck O'Malley. In casting the role McCarey obviously wanted someone who could project a priestly image but not self-righteously, and above all someone who could portray a man of the cloth without resorting to the stuffy, holier-than-thou attitude that had become such a screen stereotype.

Casting Bing Crosby in the part was a stroke of genius for McCarey. The film went on to win Academy Awards not only for itself as Best Picture, but also for Crosby as Best Actor, Barry Fitzgerald as Best Supporting Actor, and McCarey for Best Direction and Best Original Story. Although the role called upon Crosby's services as an actor first and a singer second, he sang a couple of memorable songs, including the Oscar-winning "Swingin' on a Star" and the pleasant "Day after Forever," which Crosby sang with pretty Paramount neophyte Jean Heather, appearing in the role of a cute Brooklyn singer who comes to Father O'Malley for career advice.

Like most other Hollywood triumphs, *Going My Way* paved the way for a follow-up, *The Bells of St. Mary's*, which also featured Crosby as O'Malley, as well as Ingrid Bergman as a dedicated nun who, stricken with tuberculosis, must leave her beloved post at a small parochial school. *Going My Way* established Crosby as the nation's number-one male box-office attraction, a position in which he remained longer than any other screen star in history.

But Bing Crosby's success as Father O'Malley did much more than increase his already substantial popularity as a movie personality. It also proved to both audiences and critics that he was a straight actor of definite skill. Most critics called Crosby's performance as O'Malley his best screen work. This is true; however, one cannot overlook the fact that his performance as Joe Beebe in *Sing You Sinners* had already shown that Bing possessed great ability as a dramatic actor. Unfortunately, that performance was overlooked by the press because most critics in 1938 insisted upon preserving Crosby's image as the easygoing crooner. Most of them praised the film but said very little about Bing's performance.

1945's *Here Come the Waves* reunited Crosby with *Holiday Inn* director Mark Sandrich. It remains one of the very best of the wartime musicals, containing all the beautiful zest so typical of almost all Sandrich's screen outings. Aside from the picture's quality as musical cinema, *Here Come the Waves* is also remembered as the film in which comedienne Betty Hutton gave a superb performance in the dual role of the sophisticated young lady and her scatterbrained twin sister.

Although *Going My Way* was produced by Paramount, the film's director-producer, Leo McCarey, had actually been under contract to RKO Radio for a number of years. RKO allowed McCarey to film *Going My Way* at Paramount upon the stipulation that Crosby's studio subsequently allow Bing to bring his box-office magic to a film at RKO. The film Crosby eventually made for RKO was the sequel, *The Bells of St. Mary's*.

Although the sequel never became as famous as the film that inspired it, *The Bells of St. Mary's* emerged as an excellent and witty comedy-drama. Crosby and Bergman were an effective and compelling screen team, and even though the picture copped only a single Oscar (for Sound Recording) to its predecessor's phenomenal seven, it enabled Crosby to receive his second of three Academy Award nominations and was one of RKO's most successful films of the year.

The Bells of St. Mary's brought the Father O'Malley story to a heartwarming conclusion, but in later years Paramount tried on one successful oc-

Crosby on radio's "Kraft Music Hall"

With the Andrews Sisters and Irving Berlin

casion (*Welcome Stranger*) and on another disastrous occasion (*Top o' the Morning*) to re-create the genial magic of *Going My Way* by teaming Bing Crosby and Barry Fitzgerald. However, although Crosby and Fitzgerald proved in both these films that they were to light, sugary comedy what Sydney Greenstreet and Peter Lorre were to melodrama and intrigue, they never again managed to achieve the wonderful chemistry they created as Fathers O'Malley and Fitzgibbon.

Following *Bells of St. Mary's*, Crosby returned to Paramount for one of his most flavorful and opulent screen exercises, *Blue Skies*. Reuniting Crosby, Fred Astaire, and the tunes of Irving Berlin, *Blue Skies* was a visually stunning Technicolor musical that allowed Bing and Fred to do even more singing and dancing than in *Holiday Inn*. The film was Crosby's most expensive production to date, at a budget of more than three million dollars.

1947 brought Bing his second feature with Barry Fitzgerald, *Welcome Stranger*, and the fifth and perhaps funniest *Road* picture, *Road to Rio*. The former was not in the same league with *Going My Way*, but it did contain good, solid portrayals by both Crosby and Fitzgerald and gave Crosby one superb song, "My Heart Is a Hobo." This tune was a particularly bouncy number in which Crosby explained his philosophy to Fitzgerald during a fishing jaunt. Its lyrics ideally suited Crosby's "happy wanderer" image. As in most other Crosby films, Bing is finally motivated by love to settle down.

Crosby's second film of the year, *Road to Rio*, found Bing and Bob horsing around with the Wiere Brothers in Brazil and once again vying for the love of Dorothy Lamour. Directed with skill by Norman Z. McLeod, *Road to Rio* was more perfectly structured than the other *Road* pictures. In one priceless interlude, Hope and Crosby perform a zany Samba at Dorothy Lamour's wedding party in Brazil while Crosby accompanies the Wiere Broth-

With son Gary

With Bob Hope

ers' supposedly serious Latin American instrumental backup with such ridiculous lyrics as "Everybody here likes chicken *cacciatore,* aye, aye, aye." The film was nominated for several Oscars.

Looking at the *Road* series in retrospect, it becomes apparent that the best films in the series were the second, third, fourth, and fifth and that the remaining three are merely average screen comedies that don't come up to the high standard of hilarity established by *Zanzibar, Morocco, Utopia,* and *Rio.* Of course, it is relatively easy to see why the first film of the series, *Road to Singapore,* failed to measure up to the later pictures. The first movie was an experiment for both Crosby and Hope, and the wacky format that was to play such an important part in the later films had not yet been created. Moreover, it is fairly sure that neither Paramount nor Bing and Bob had the vaguest idea that such a modest little film would one day inspire a series. The film was a somewhat less-than-sensational comedy, but it showed definitely that Hope and Crosby worked beautifully together.

1947's *The Emperor Waltz* remains one of Bing Crosby's most thoroughly charming musical films. A large-scale Technicolor production directed by screen veteran Billy Wilder, it features Joan Fontaine as a spoiled Austrian countess who is romanced by a tough little phonograph salesman from America (Bing). "The Emperor Waltz" is in many ways a beautiful motion-picture experience. The rather ordinary story of the poor man falling in love with the rich girl here becomes a unique film that never gives way to soggy, cornball sentiment. This film presented moviegoers with a great many visual delights (such as Hans Drier's incredible set for the ballroom in the emperor's palace) and some delightfully absurd tongue-in-cheek episodes like the one in which an entire Tyrolean village (in which all the inhabitants are virtuoso violinists) pulsates with the poignant melodies of Heuberger's

"Chambre Separée" to get Crosby and Fontaine in a romantic mood. The movie was particularly popular among film audiences of 1947 because it depicted a beautiful and seemingly unattainable countess (Fontaine) falling in love with a rather ordinary-looking man (Crosby) whose only "noble" quality was his honesty. For one of the first times on screen, a studio produced a love story wherein the man was a very common, easygoing guy who didn't resemble Errol Flynn or Alan Ladd and wasn't tough like Bogart or Cagney but who could still win the love of a beautiful woman.

Crosby's next screen vehicle, every bit as charming and lavish as *The Emperor Waltz*, was an entertaining modernization of Mark Twain's *A Connecticut Yankee in King Arthur's Court*. The film featured Crosby as the "Yankee" who travels back through the centuries, to encounter King Arthur (Sir Cedric Hardwicke) and his knights Sir Lancelot, Sir Galahad, and Sir Sagrimore. Bing's Yankee also runs across a beautiful maiden named Lady Alesande (Rhonda Fleming) and, as is to be expected, soon falls in love with her.

This film resembles *The Emperor Waltz* in that it presents Crosby as an easygoing "nice guy" who finds himself suddenly thrust into the presence of royalty and becomes the heart's desire of a beautiful woman of quality. Although none of the songs from *A Connecticut Yankee* became hits, Bing's tunes in the film were cheerful. One of them, a delightful little number called "There's Nothing to Be Ashamed of If You Stub Your Toe on the Moon," is one of Bing's cutest screen ditties. This film, Bing Crosby's last "classic" musical, marked the end of the performer's most productive and fruitful period as a film personality.

In late 1948, Crosby began his affiliation with Minute Maid Orange Juice by becoming a large stockholder in the Vacuum Foods Corporation. To this day, he is frequently seen in television commer-

With Tallulah Bankhead

With Cecil B. DeMille and Bob Hope

With Jack Benny

cials for the product in which he and his second wife, Kathryn Grant, as well as the three younger Crosbys (Harry, Nathaniel, and Mary) sing the praises of Minute Maid Orange Juice.

Crosby's next two films for Paramount, *Top o' the Morning* and *Mr. Music*, were both disappointing. The always enjoyable presence of Barry Fitzgerald in the former did nothing to counterbalance that picture's surprising lack of quality.

Somewhat better was *Riding High*, Frank Capra's charming tale of life among the horseplayers, in which Crosby appeared as the manager of a faithful colt named Broadway Bill. The film was such an enormous box-office success and was so well received by both audiences and critics that it paved the way for a second Crosby-Capra picture, *Here Comes the Groom*, which turned out to be even better than *Riding High*. Among other things, it contained an excellent song by Johnny Mercer and Hoagy Carmichael, "In the Cool, Cool, Cool of the Evening." It also boasted a superb supporting cast featuring Jane Wyman, Alexis Smith, and Franchot Tone.

Following *Here Comes the Groom*, Crosby made two screen appearances in 1952, opposite Jane Wyman in the pleasant *Just for You* and opposite his old pal Bob Hope in the sixth and last of the Paramount *Road* series, *Road to Bali*. Both were enjoyable Technicolor productions featuring good songs and impressive supporting casts but lacking much of the old-time magic.

Crosby's first dramatic role with no tinges of comedy was in George Seaton's excellent 1953 production, *Little Boy Lost*. A gripping account of a war correspondent's desperate search through the streets of war-torn Paris for his lost child, the picture was one of the few Crosby films shot on location. The picture featured Bing in a role that was a forerunner to his later, and perhaps best, dramatic work in *The Country Girl*.

But before Crosby undertook that assignment, he returned to musicals in a big, expensive production named for his most successful single recording, "White Christmas." A superbly produced picture containing a generous amount of clowning by Crosby, Danny Kaye, Rosemary Clooney, and Vera-Ellen, *White Christmas* was a tremendous financial success, but it is of little interest to most film students except for the fact that it was the first film shot in VistaVision.

In late 1954, Crosby again joined forces with George Seaton and William Perlberg (the director and producer, respectively, of *Little Boy Lost*) on a heavily dramatic film of the successful Clifford Odets play *The Country Girl*. Bing here offered his finest film performance as the alcoholic actor protagonist. For his portrayal in *The Country Girl*, Crosby received his third Academy Award nomination for Best Actor. Although he didn't win the Oscar (Marlon Brando did, for *On the Waterfront*), Bing did receive a citation as Best Actor of the Year from the National Board of Review.

Unfortunately, Crosby's next picture, *Anything Goes,* was unworthy of Crosby's presence. It emerged as one of the performer's weakest all-around motion pictures.

Winding up his long association with Paramount in 1956, Crosby ventured into the one entertainment medium in which he had yet to make his mark, appearing on television in the Maxwell Anderson play *High Tor,* opposite Julie Andrews. Although this venture was successful for Crosby, it is interesting to note that his attempt to establish a weekly series (1964's short-lived "The Bing Crosby Show") was curiously unsuccessful. Crosby's greatest success on the tube has been as a sort of "every-so-often" master of ceremonies (such as on "The Hollywood Palace") or as a producer (of such important and long-running shows as "Ben Casey") or as the star of annual Christmas specials in which he

With sons Phil, Lindsay, Gary and Dennis

With Judy Garland

With High Society *co-star Grace Kelly*

always sings the favorite "White Christmas." These Christmas specials have been extremely popular with TV viewers, and Crosby still does a Yuletide special each year. Bing's wife, Kathryn, and children Harry, Nathaniel, and Mary have joined him and proved that vocal talent is not limited to the most famous member of the household.

1956's *High Society* was Bing Crosby's first film for MGM since *Going Hollywood* in 1933. This colorful, well-produced picture cast Crosby opposite Frank Sinatra, the man who succeeded him as the popular music world's most important personality. The two worked well together.

Crosby stayed at MGM for 1957's *Man on Fire*, another of Bing's memorable straight-acting assignments and one of the three Crosby vehicles (the other two were *Stagecoach* in 1966 and *Doctor Cook's Garden* in 1971) in which the performer did not sing. *Man on Fire* was a straight drama of genuine merit. Crosby's performance amply demonstrated that he possessed an almost infallible intuition as an actor that many critics have stubbornly refused to acknowledge. Unfortunately, Crosby would get very few other chances to display his acting abilities in his remaining screen vehicles.

His next four films, *Say One for Me*, *High Time*, *The Road to Hong Kong*, and *Robin and the Seven Hoods,* were far below Crosby's usual standard. Even the best of them, *High Time,* was a disappointment to most Crosby fans. It was, however, an entertaining large-scale production in which Bing undertook the amusing role of a rich, middle-aged owner of a restaurant chain who surprises his grown children by enrolling in college as a freshman.

In 1966, Crosby, undertook another dramatic role as the alcoholic physician Dr. Josiah Boone in the lavish 20th Century-Fox remake of John Ford's *Stagecoach*. Although the Doc Boone role was certainly demanding and allowed Crosby to succeed at a very difficult kind of seriocomic characterization

On the High Society *set with Barrett Deems*

as a hopeless drunkard, most moviegoers who remembered the 1939 John Ford film didn't take to this high-budgeted remake. Nevertheless, Bing Crosby's superbly controlled performance as Doctor Boone remains as one of his most fascinating movie portrayals.

Even more fascinating, however, was Crosby's last film role to date in the 1971 television movie, *Dr. Cook's Garden*. One of the better television movies, this film featured Crosby in one of the most unusual roles of his career. Playing the role of a genial yet psychopathic doctor who believes that the best way to eliminate disease is to dispose of the ill, Crosby turned in a surprisingly chilling performance. Demonstrating that he is as versatile as he is talented, Crosby made his Dr. Cook into a unique and refreshing departure from the norm. He also made it next to impossible for the audience to comprehend that this was the very same Bing Crosby who had delighted filmgoers with his cheerful portrayals of past decades.

Although Dr. Cook is the most villainous character Crosby has ever played, he is nevertheless able to evoke a great deal of sympathy by showing Doctor Cook as a man driven to commit his hideous crimes by some dark, unknown force deep within him. As a result, Crosby gives the audience the feeling that Dr. Cook is the victim of a devastating mental disorder. Because of this, the viewer is naturally repelled by what Doctor Cook does but cannot help but feel a tinge of pity for the character.

Bing Crosby's first wife, Dixie Lee, died in 1952, shortly after the completion of *Little Boy Lost*. In 1957 he married the former Kathryn Grandstaff of Houston, known for a time in the screen world as Kathryn Grant. They first encountered each other on the Paramount lot in 1954 while Bing was preparing to make *White Christmas*. Although it was definitely love at first sight, Bing and Kathryn

With wife Kathryn Grant at 1954 Oscar ceremony

With son Harry, wife Kathryn, son Nathaniel and daughter Mary

Bing Crosby, *his wife* Kathryn *(left), daughter* Mary Frances *and sons* Nathaniel *(left) and* Harry Lillis Jr. *on "Bing Crosby's White Christmas Special," November, 1976*

didn't manage to reach the altar for three years, mostly because many people felt that Crosby shouldn't marry a woman so much younger than he. But in 1957, love finally conquered, and the two were married in Las Vegas.

Mrs. Crosby later flourished as a film and stage actress of considerable skill and beauty in films like *The Seventh Voyage of Sinbad* and especially in *Anatomy of a Murder* and most recently with San Francisco's famous repertory company, the American Conservatory Theatre. She has also become the mother of three children, Harry III, Mary Frances, and Nathaniel, and she published a book, *Bing and Other Things,* in 1967. Mrs. Crosby, who seems to grow more beautiful with the passage of time, also appeared on television in the American Conservatory Theatre's production of *Cyrano De Bergerac* (in which she portrayed Lise) on the PBS series "Theatre in America."

Except for his Christmas specials and occasional appearances on television variety shows, Bing Crosby has, like many other performers from Hollywood's Golden Era, chosen to stay out of the spotlight of show business in recent years. He seems content to live in "semi-retirement."

On January 13, 1974, he underwent major surgery to remove a large fungus that had invaded his left lung. Happily, Crosby recovered nicely from the operation.

His semi-retirement has, of course, made it possible for Bing to do all the things he likes the most, such as hunting, fishing, and golfing. The November 1973 issue of *Field and Stream* carried a lengthy article describing Crosby's prowess as a hunter and fisherman.

With Bing Crosby now living the sort of life that one would expect a "retired" giant of show business to live, it seems hard to believe that only twenty-odd years ago he was an important and beloved star. Yet even though he is no longer active as a film personality, his legend looms larger than ever, thanks largely to the frequent revivals of his movies (particularly the forties musicals) on television and the constant rereleasing of his old recording hits.

As a result, a whole new generation is learning about the special brand of Crosby magic and the wonderful aura that surrounds the performer in virtually everything he does. Whether he plays comedy, satire, or straight drama, the magic is always there, as indestructible as the Crosby legend. Long after the cynicism of a great deal of today's cinema is forgotten, films like *Going My Way* will continue to be watched, studied, and enjoyed, not only because they were extremely entertaining stories, but also because their brand of schmaltz is extremely palatable. The best of the Crosby films represent a wonderful, compelling innocence and charm that communicates its simple message to audiences without blatant sentiment or heart tugging.

The popularity and success of the video revivals of Bing Crosby films puts a rather ironic capper on the Crosby legend, illustrating how the one entertainment medium Bing never truly conquered is now indirectly making him popular all over again.

With wife Kathryn Grant

Bing Crosby's Academy Award-Winning and Academy Award-Nominated Songs

(The following list of songs were all sung by
Bing Crosby in a particular film and were either
nominated for an Oscar or won the coveted prize.
The Oscar-winning songs in this list are the
titles which are italicized.)

1   "LOVE IN BLOOM" from the film "SHE LOVES ME NOT" 1934
2   "PENNIES FROM HEAVEN" from the film "PENNIES FROM HEAVEN" 1936
3   *"SWEET LEILANI"* from the film "WAIKIKI WEDDING" 1937
4   "ONLY FOREVER" from the film "RHYTHM ON THE RIVER" 1940
5   *"WHITE CHRISTMAS"* from the film "HOLIDAY INN" 1942
6   *"SWINGIN' ON A STAR"* from the film "GOING MY WAY" 1944
7   "ACCENTUATE THE POSITIVE" from the film "HERE COMES THE WAVES" 1945
8   "AREN'T YOU GLAD YOU'RE YOU?" from the film "THE BELLS OF
     ST. MARY'S" 1945
9   "YOU KEEP COMING BACK LIKE A SONG" from the film "BLUE SKIES" 1946
10 *"IN THE COOL, COOL, COOL OF THE EVENING"* from the film
     "HERE COMES THE GROOM" 1951
11 "ZING A LITTLE ZONG" from the film "JUST FOR YOU" 1952
12 "COUNT YOUR BLESSINGS" from the film "WHITE CHRISTMAS" 1954
13 "TRUE LOVE" from the film "HIGH SOCIETY" 1956
14 "THE SECOND TIME AROUND" from the film "HIGH TIME" 1960

Crosby at the Box Office

(As an illustration of Bing Crosby's popularity as a film star during his peak era, this list of film titles represents those Crosby films which were listed among the largest grossing motion pictures of the year.

1. *"SHE LOVES ME NOT"* (Paramount, 1934)
2. *"RHYTHM ON THE RANGE"* (Paramount, 1936)
3. *"WAIKIKI WEDDING"* (Paramount, 1937)
4. *"ROAD TO SINGAPORE"* (Paramount, 1940)
5. *"ROAD TO ZANZIBAR"* (Paramount, 1941)
6. *"HOLIDAY INN"* (Paramount, 1942)
7. *"ROAD TO MOROCCO"* (Paramount, 1942)
8. *"STAR-SPANGLED RHYTHM"* (Paramount, 1943)
9. *"DIXIE"* (Paramount, 1943)
10. *"GOING MY WAY"* (Paramount, 1944)
11. *"HERE COMES THE WAVES"* (Paramount, 1945)
12. *"DUFFY'S TAVERN"* (Paramount, 1945)
13. *"BELLS OF ST. MARY'S"* (RKO, 1945)
14. *"ROAD TO UTOPIA"* (Paramount, 1946)
15. *"BLUE SKIES"* (Paramount, 1946)
16. *"WELCOME STRANGER"* (Paramount, 1947)
17. *"ROAD TO RIO"* (Paramount, 1947)
18. *"THE EMPEROR WALTZ"* (Paramount, 1948)
19. *"A CONNECTICUT YANKEE IN KING ARTHUR'S COURT"* (Paramount, 1949)
20. *"HERE COMES THE GROOM"* (Paramount, 1951)
21. *"JUST FOR YOU"* (Paramount, 1952)
22. *"ROAD TO BALI"* (Paramount, 1953)
23. *"LITTLE BOY LOST"* (Paramount, 1953)
24. *"WHITE CHRISTMAS"* (Paramount, 1954)
25. *"THE COUNTRY GIRL"* (Paramount, 1954)
26. *"HIGH SOCIETY"* (MGM, 1956)
27. *"SAY ONE FOR ME"* (20th Century Fox, 1959)
28. *"THE ROAD TO HONG KONG"* (United Artists, 1962)
29. *"ROBIN AND THE HOODS"* (Warner Brothers, 1964)

The Big Broadcast

1932

CAST

Bing Hornsby (BING CROSBY); Leslie McWhinney (STU ERWIN); Anita Rogers (*Leila* HYAMS); Mona (*Sharon Lynne*); George (*George Burns*); Gracie (*Gracie Allen*); Clapsaddle (*George Barbier*); Announcer (*Ralph Robertson*); Animal Man (*Alex Melish*); Boy (*Spec O'Donnell*); Mrs. Cohen (*Anna Chandler*); Officer (*Tom Carrigan*).

CREDITS

A Paramount Publix Picture. Directed by Frank Tuttle. Screenplay by George Marion, Jr. Based on the play *Wild Waves,* by William Ford Manley. Director of Photography: George Folsey. Songs by Ralph Rainger and Leo Robin.

SONGS

"Here Lies Love"
"Please"
"Where the Blue of the Night Meets the Gold of the Day"

Running Time: 80 minutes

The Big Broadcast of 1932 was a Hollywood attempt to scoop the radio industry by featuring a number of radio's most popular performers in a film dealing with the broadcasting industry in a humorous and light-hearted manner. Hollywood hoped to gain the attention of a sizable portion of its fiercest competitor's massive audience by offering radio buffs the opportunity to see Bing Crosby, George Burns, Gracie Allen, Kate Smith, Arthur Tracy, the Mills Brothers, the Boswell Sisters, and Cab Calloway on the screen.

Much to Hollywood's delight, the film audiences of the day fell head over heels in love with *The Big Broadcast,* and although some critics panned the film for being too unusual and innovative, it became a tremendous box-office success. The film was, in fact, so successful that it inspired an entire series of *Big Broadcast* pictures, all of which were enter-

With Leila Hyams and Stuart Erwin

taining, even though none of them surpassed the original in terms of entertainment value. In addition to being a truly first-rate musical-comedy revue, the original *Big Broadcast* also rates a special niche in the annals of film history because it was the picture mostly responsible for catapulting Bing Crosby into screen stardom.

The plot of *The Big Broadcast* is an admittedly incidental little affair whose sole purpose is to pave the way for the crooning of Bing Crosby; the frequently hilarious comedic interludes featuring George Burns, Gracie Allen, and Stuart Erwin; and the impressive guest shots by the other radio performers. It revolves, of course, around a radio station, managed by Burns, that features the talents of crooning heart throb Crosby. The main problem in the story is that the easygoing Bing seems as irresponsible as he is talented, and this naturally causes great concern at the station until the predictably happy finale.

A mildly impressive debut for Bing Crosby in a feature-length movie, *The Big Broadcast* doesn't really allow the performer to do very much in terms of character development, but it was apparent that the youthful crooner would one day emerge as a front-ranking film personality. Even in this film, it was evident that, like every other popular screen star, Bing Crosby possessed that elusive and indefinable personality dimension known as "star quality."

Oddly, the first of the *Broadcast* movies served as the springboard for Bing Crosby's film career, and the last of them did much the same for another talented young radio personality named Bob Hope.

With Mary Carlisle

College Humor

1933

CAST

Professor Frederick Danvers (BING CROSBY); Barney Shirrel (JACK OAKIE); Barbara Shirrel (*Mary CARLISLE*); Mondrake (*Richard ARLEN*); Amber (*Mary Kornmann*); George (*George Burns*); Gracie (*Gracie Allen*); Ginger (*Lona Andre*); Tex (*Joseph Sawyer*).

CREDITS

A Paramount Picture. Directed by Wesley Ruggles. Adapted for the Screen by Claude Binyon and Frank Butler. Based on a Story by Dean Fales.

Director of Photography: Leo Tover, A.S.C. Songs by Arthur Johnston and Sam Coslow.

SONGS

"The Old Ox Road"
"Learn to Croon"
"Play Ball"
"Moonstruck"

Running Time: 68 minutes

College Humor is an enjoyable little mixture of songs and comedy in which Professor Bing Crosby is actively pursued by a beautiful young coed (Mary Carlisle), much to the chagrin of the resident "Big Man on Campus," Richard Arlen.

The film was just one of many "college" pictures Hollywood produced during the thirties. The most popular campus films were *College Holiday, Horse-feathers, Girls Demand Excitement, Life Begins in College, Hold 'Em Yale, Varsity Show, College Coach, College Rhythm,* and *College Humor*. Of course, most of these films are impossible to enjoy today, but *College Humor* has withstood the test of time and seems as entertaining today as it was forty-odd years ago. The principal reason for this is that *College Humor* does not approach its some-what colorless subject in a very serious manner. Although the film contains all the standard ingredients of a typically campy thirties college picture (including a trumped-up, glorified football game in the final reel), *College Humor* and the Marx Brothers' brilliant *Horsefeathers* are perhaps the only two college films produced during the thirties that can still be enjoyed and appreciated.

College Humor owes almost all its effectiveness to the guiding hand of director Wesley Ruggles. Realizing that his subject matter could easily have emerged on screen as cute and corny, Ruggles wisely elected to approach the material in a very light and humorous fashion. The director's approach to the film is nicely reflected in the performances of all cast members, most notably Bing Crosby as the romantic scholar with the golden voice, Richard Arlen as the campus bigshot and varsity football star, and especially George Burns and Gracie Allen as the operators of a nutty catering service.

With Richard Arlen and Jack Oakie

Too Much Harmony

1933

CAST

Eddie Bronson (BING CROSBY); Benny Day (JACK OAKIE); Ruth Brown (*Judith* ALLEN); Johnny Dixon (*Skeets Gallagher*); Max Merlin (*Harry Green*); Lucille Watson (*Lilyan Tashman*); Lem (*Ned Sparks*); Patsy Dugan (*Kitty Kelly*); Verne La Mont (*Grace Bradley*); Mrs. Gallotti (*Anna Demetrio*); Mrs. Day (*Evelyn Oakie*); Stage Director (*Billy Bevan*); Lilyan (*Shirley Grey*).

CREDITS

A Paramount Picture. Directed by Edward Sutherland. Original Story by Joseph L. Mankiewicz. Dialogue by Harry Ruskin. Songs by Sam Coslow and Arthur Johnston.

Running Time: 76 minutes

A mildly enjoyable but thoroughly plotless formula picture, *Too Much Harmony* tells the tale of an easygoing crooner (Crosby) and the two women in his life, one a good girl (Judith Allen) and the other a bad one (Lilyan Tashman). This is one of those Hollywood curios that are seldom if ever shown these days because their appeal is extremely limited.

Not nearly as well produced as *Big Broadcast* and

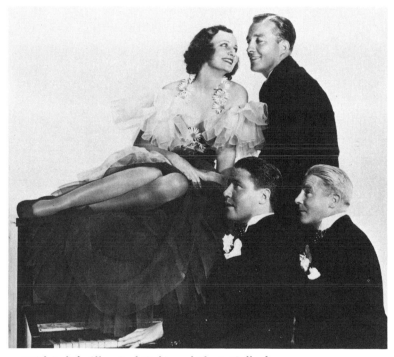

With Judith Allen, Jack Oakie and Skeets Gallagher

containing none of the sharp comedic interludes that had made *College Humor* so entertaining, *Too Much Harmony* is old-fashioned and hopelessly outdated, if somehow charming. It would probably have been banished to some dark corner of a dusty film archive if it hadn't been one of Crosby's earliest screen vehicles and therefore valuable to film history. *Too Much Harmony* remains one of Crosby's weakest apprentice efforts.

The film was directed by screen veteran Edward Sutherland, who would later guide Crosby through *Mississippi*, his memorable "field day" with W. C. Fields, and through one of his best major films, *Dixie*.

Going Hollywood

1933

CAST

Bill Williams (BING CROSBY); Sylvia (MARION DAVIES); Lili Yvonne (FIFI D'ORSAY); Ernest (*Stuart* ERWIN); Jill (*Patsy Kelly*); Jack Thompson (*Bobby Watson*); Bert (*Ned Sparks*).

CREDITS

A Metro-Goldwyn-Mayer Production. Directed by Raoul Walsh. Adapted for the Screen by Donald Ogden Stewart. From an Original Story by Frances Marion. Director of Photography: George Folsey. Musical Director: Lennie Hayton. Songs by Nacio Brown and Arthur Freed.

SONGS

"Temptation"
"We'll Make Love When It Rains"
"Our Big Love Scene"

Running Time: 75 minutes

With Marion Davies

Largely forgotten today, *Going Hollywood* is of interest to the student of film history primarily because it was one of the few good motion pictures in which Marion Davies was allowed to star. The film was a light, unpretentious little musical comedy that seemed to work better for Marion than did her more serious dramatic vehicles. The film's plot was typical of those of most Bing Crosby screen vehicles of the 1930s—a simple and lightly told Hollywood success story wherein an avid and adoring fan (Marion) falls hopelessly in love with her favorite show-business personality (Bing) and one day finds herself signed on as his leading lady.

Going Hollywood is also of interest because it was directed by Raoul Walsh, who in just a few short years would become one of the most respected filmmakers in the industry. Proving that he could handle an innocuous little comedy with the same skill that he brought to his later classics, Walsh wrapped *Going Hollywood* up into a pleasant package, a fun-filled combination of music and comedy.

This was the film in which Bing sang one of his most famous and effective torch tunes, "Temptation."

With Marion Davies

We're Not Dressing

1934

CAST

Steve Jones (BING CROSBY); Doris Worthington (CAROLE LOMBARD); George (*George* BURNS); Gracie (*Gracie* ALLEN); Edith (*Ethel Merman*); Hubert (*Leon Errol*); Prince Michael (*Raymond Milland*); Prince Alexander (*Jay Henry*); Old Sailor (*John Irwin*); Captain (*Charles Morris*); First Officer (*Ben Hendricks*); Second Officer (*Ted Oliver*).

CREDITS

A Paramount Picture. Directed by Norman Taurog. Associate Producer: Benjamin Glazer. Screenplay by Horace Jackson, George Marion, Jr., and Francis Martin. From an Original Story by Benjamin Glazer. Based on the Play by Sir J. M. Barrie. Director of Photography: Charles Lang, A.S.C. Songs by Mack Gordon and Harry Revel.

SONGS

''Love Thy Neighbor''
''She Reminds Me of You''
''Riding Round in the Rain''
''Good Night, Lovely Little Lady''
''May I?''
''Once in a Blue Moon''

Running Time: 80 minutes

With Carole Lombard

With Carole Lombard

With L. to R., Leon Errol, Ethel Merman, Jay Henry, Carole Lombard, and Ray Milland

As a refreshing change of pace from straight musicals, Paramount cast Crosby in the lead in *We're Not Dressing,* a musical-comedy adaptation of J. M. Barrie's popular play *The Admirable Crichton.* The film also featured such topnotch performers as Carole Lombard, Leon Errol, Ethel Merman, George Burns, and Gracie Allen. Released in 1934, the adaptation was only vaguely faithful to Barrie's seriocomic tale of how a quirk of fate allows a butler to become the master of the family he has been serving when the family is shipwrecked on a God-forsaken island and must depend upon the resourcefulness of the butler for its survival.

We're Not Dressing was a bright and breezy musical comedy, the most entertaining screen vehicle in which Bing Crosby had appeared. In addition to presenting Crosby with the opportunity to bring his excellent vocal interpretation to no fewer than five superb songs, *We're Not Dressing* also enabled him to display his agreeable style as a light comedian.

A most enjoyable screen vehicle for both Bing Crosby and Carole Lombard (appearing as an unattainable millionairess who finally loses her heart to the modest crooner), *We're Not Dressing* was just one of several highly successful film adaptations of Barrie's remarkably flexible play. An earlier screen version entitled *Male and Female* adhered very closely to the Barrie original and contained superb performances by Gloria Swanson and Thomas Meighan under the direction of Cecil B. DeMille. Several decades after the DeMille treatment, *The Admirable Crichton* also served as the basis for two extremely well-produced British films, one of which was directed in the early fifties by Noel Langley. *We're Not Dressing* is perhaps the most imaginative version of them all, even though it may have been a bit wackier than Sir J. M. Barrie would have liked.

With Edward Nugent, Miriam Hopkins and Lynne Overman

She Loves Me Not

1934

CAST

Paul Lawton (BING CROSBY); Curly Flagg (MIRIAM HOPKINS); Buzz Jones (*Edward* NUGENT); Midge Mercer (*Kitty* CARLISLE); Dean Mercer (*Henry Stephenson*); Gus McNeal (*Lynne Overman*); Mugg (*Warren Hymer*); Frances (*Judith Allen*); J. Thorval Jones (*George Barbier*); Charles Lawton (*Henry Kolker*); Martha (*Margaret Armstrong*); Mrs. Arbuthnot (*Maude Gordon*); J. B. (*Ralf Harolde*); Andy (*Matt McHugh*).

CREDITS

A Paramount Picture. Directed by Elliot Nugent. Produced by Benjamin Glazer. Screenplay by Benjamin Glazer. Based on the Play by Howard Lindsay. From the Novel by Edward Hope. Director of Photography: Charles Lang, A.S.C. Set Decoration: A. E. Fruedeman. Costume Supervision: Edith Head. Film Editor: Hugh Bennett.

SONGS

"Love in Bloom," by Ralph Rainger and Leo Robin
Other Songs by Harry Revel, Mack Gordon, Edward Heyman, and Arthur Schwartz

Running Time: 83 minutes

With Henry Stephenson, Miriam Hopkins and Lynne Overman

It is generally acknowledged that many Bing Crosby films of the 1930s were little more than springboards for five or six popular songs. In films like *Too Much Harmony, Here Is My Heart, Two for Tonight, Pennies from Heaven*, and *Doctor Rhythm*, it seemed as if the performer was forced to wade through ninety minutes of silliness for the sole purpose of crooning such fanciful ballads as "Please," "Love Is Just around the Corner," "It's June in January," "From the Top of Your Head to the Tip of Your Toes," and "One, Two, Button My Shoe." Although most critics of the day found this type of entertainment mildly diverting, they almost all preferred Crosby in films with a fairly inventive plotline, in addition to romantic songs. One of the best examples of such a film was 1934's *She Loves Me Not,* a skillfully written Crosby vehicle that contains one of the more clever plotlines conceived for a light musical comedy.

The film revolves around Bing Crosby and Edward Nugent as a couple of affable prep students at Princeton who find themselves giving sanctuary to a pretty murder witness (Miriam Hopkins). Since the college dean (Henry Stephenson) wouldn't take it too kindly if he found out about Miriam, Crosby and Nugent decide to disguise Miriam as a man. This, of course, sets the stage for some lively comedy situations, and what emerges is a brisk and expertly produced vehicle that never fails to amuse while providing Crosby with an opportunity to sharpen his budding skill as a comedian.

Based on the popular play by Howard Lindsay, *She Loves Me Not* has held up well over the years. Its madcap humor and witty dialogue seem every bit as fresh and entertaining today as they did then. In fact, *She Loves Me Not* is probably one of the few sound comedies produced before 1935 that has not lost any of its original punch.

With Miriam Hopkins

Here Is My Heart
1934

CAST

J. Paul Jones (BING CROSBY); Princess Alexandra (KITTY CARLISLE); Prince Nickolas (ROLAND YOUNG); Countess Rostova (ALISON SKIPWORTH); Prince Vladimir (*Reginald* OWEN); Suzette (*Cecelia Parker*); James Smith (*William Frawley*); Claire (*Marian Mansfield*); Hotel Manager (*Akim Tamiroff*); Higgins (*Charles Arnt*); Waiter (*Arthur Housman*); Captain (*Charles Wilson*); Secretary (*Cromwell McKechnie*).

CREDITS

A Paramount Picture. Directed by Frank Tuttle. Produced by Louis D. Lighton. Screenplay by Edwin Justus Mayer and Harlan Thompson. Based on the Play *The Grand Duchess and the Waiter*, by Alfred Savoir. Director of Photography: Karl Struss, A.S.C. Songs by Leo Robin, Ralph Rainger, and Lewis Gensler.

SONGS

"Love Is Just around the Corner"
"June in January"
"With Every Breath I Take"

Running Time: 75 minutes

Here Is My Heart is one of several successful motion pictures presenting Bing Crosby in the role of a nice, ordinary fellow who dares to pitch woo at a beautiful, high-class woman who usually wants nothing to do with him. The film is actually a forerunner to the later *The Emperor Waltz* in that it casts Bing in the role of an easygoing American chap who ventures to a foreign country and loses his heart to a blueblooded member of a royal family. In *Here Is My Heart*, Crosby appears as a wealthy and famous crooner who disguises himself as an efficient waiter to get closer to an unattainable princess (Kitty Carlisle).

Crosby's preceding two screen vehicles, *We're Not Dressing* and *She Loves Me Not*, had enabled the performer to polish his acting technique, and the results are plainly apparent here. His reactions, timing, and delivery are so perfect that it is almost impossible to believe that Crosby had once seemed uncomfortable in front of the camera.

Even though he was playing against such veteran actors as Roland Young, Alison Skipworth, and Reginald Owen, Crosby dominated the film with his excellent comic portrayal of the romantic and adventurous crooner. Director Frank Tuttle keeps Crosby on his toes throughout, and the scenes in which Bing masquerades as a waiter have a definite comedic flair. Under Tuttle's direction, Crosby also overcomes many of the improbabilities of the film's script and is thus able to make much of the film's silliness seem palatable.

With William Frawley

Mississippi
1935

CAST

Tom Grayson (BING CROSBY); Commodore Jackson (W. C. FIELDS); Lucy Rumford (JOAN BENNETT); Elvira (*Gail Patrick*); Alabam (*Queenie Smith*); Gerald (*Claude Gillingwater*); Major Patterson (*John Miljan*); Joe Patterson (*Ed Pawley*); Captain Blackie (*Fred Kohler*); Lavinia (*Libby Taylor*); Stage Manager (*Harry Meyers*); Rumbo (*John Larkin*); Hefty (*Paul Hurst*); First Gambler (*King Baggott*); Second Gambler (*Mahlon Hamilton*); Miss Markham (*Theresa Conover*); Colonel (*Bruce Covington*); Hotel Manager (*Clarence Geldert*); Bartender (*Jules Cowles*).

CREDITS

A Paramount Picture. Directed by Edward A. Sutherland. Produced by Arthur Hornblow, Jr. Screenplay by Jack Cunningham and Francis Martin. Adapted from Booth Tarkington's *Magnolia*. Adaptation by Claude Binyon, Herbert Fields, Jack Cunningham, and Frances Martin. Director of Photography: Charles Lang, A.S.C. Songs by Richard Rodgers and Lorenz Hart.

SONGS

"Down by the River"
"Soon"
"Easy to Remember But So Hard to Forget"

Running Time: 75 minutes

Mississippi, a major comedy classic of the 1930s, is also a particular favorite among the admirers of both Bing Crosby and W. C. Fields. The film, an expensive and lavishly produced adaptation of Booth Tarkington's *Magnolia,* tells the story of a peace-loving young man who refuses to conform to the old South's practice of dueling. This splendid combination of comedy, music, and adventure gives Crosby and Fields opportunity to show their talents off to the best possible advantage.

Although most film buffs remember *Mississippi* primarily as a Fields vehicle, Crosby fans have always looked upon it as a particularly intriguing part of Bing's career because it allows him to engage in a truly convincing rough-and-tumble saloon brawl with veteran screen heavy Fred Kohler. Thus, *Mississippi* is one of the few Crosby films that enables the performer to show that he could be as handy with his fists as with his voice.

The film begins as Tom Grayson (Bing Crosby) becomes a member of a theatrical showboat company after being disgraced by his fiancée's family for his pacifism. The leader of the company, Commodore Jackson (W. C. Fields), immediately recognizing Tom's singing abilities, soon turns the young man into the featured attraction aboard the showboat.

All goes well for Tom until a black-hearted river rat, Captain Blackie (Fred Kohler), disrupts one of his performances and forces the lad into a furious saloon fight. During the brawl, Captain Blackie is accidentally shot with his own pistol, and Tom subsequently gains a reputation as the fellow who single-handedly disposed of one of the most notorious villains of the river.

Taking advantage of Tom's sudden fame, Commodore Jackson begins advertising the young troubadour as Colonel Blake, the Singing Killer. This

With Joe Morrison, Queenie Smith and Edward Sutherland

title pleases everyone but Lucy Rumford (Joan Bennett), the younger sister of Tom's former fiancée, who has been secretly in love with Grayson for months. Realizing that he reciprocates her affection, Tom tries to explain to Lucy that the Singing Killer title wasn't his idea, but she wants nothing to do with a man with such a notorious reputation. Before long, however, Tom manages to win Lucy back, and the final scene shows the young couple locked in an affectionate embrace aboard Commodore Jackson's riverboat.

Mississippi also received excellent attention from the expert camera of cinematographer Charles Lang. Employing beautiful, soft, and glistening black-and-white photography, Lang made the film superb visual entertainment as well as a comedy classic.

Bing Crosby gives a smooth performance as the suave riverboat romeo and delivers his songs in a sincere manner. But it is W. C. Fields and his repertoire of matchless comedy routines that admittedly carry the greater weight of the film. Particularly memorable is the scene in which crooked poker dealer Fields mistakenly gives himself five aces and quickly tries to rectify the matter when he sees that his four opponents look as though they wouldn't be at all averse to shedding his blood. The priceless gimmick of the scene is that every card Fields subsequently draws is also an ace!

With W. C. Fields

With Joan Bennett

With Fred Kohler

With Thelma Todd, Mary Boland, Lynne Overman and Joan Bennett

Two for Tonight

1935

CAST

Gilbert Gordon (BING CROSBY); Bobbie Lockwood (JOAN BENNETT); Harry (*Lynne* OVERMAN); Mrs. Smythe (*Mary* BOLAND); Lilly (*Thelma* TODD); Buster Da Costa (*James Blakeley*); Pooch Donahue (*Douglas Fowley*); Alexander (*Maurice* Cass); Homps (*Ernest Cossart*); Writer (*Charles Lane*); Benny (*Charles Arnt*); Jailer (*A. S. Byron*); Prisoner (*John Gough*).

CREDITS

A Paramount Picture. Directed by Frank Tuttle. Screenplay by George Marion, Jr., and Jane Storm. Based on a Play by Max Lief and J. O. Lief. Additional Dialogue by Harry Ruskin. Director of Photography: Karl Struss, A.S.C. Songs by Mack Gordon and Harry Revel.

SONGS

"I Wish I Were Aladdin"
"Without a Word of Warning"
"From the Top of Your Head to the Tip of Your Toes"
"Takes Two to Make a Bargain"

Running Time: 61 minutes

Two for Tonight is a minor picture that stands as an example of how even the best and most talented cast can be hopelessly bogged down by a poor vehicle. A slickly produced but truly absurd musical comedy featuring Bing Crosby, Joan Bennett, Mary Boland, and Thelma Todd, the film deals foolishly with the story of a gifted young tunesmith (Crosby) who undertakes the monumental task of concocting a full-length theatrical piece within a few days.

As if the film's ridiculous plot weren't enough to paralyze Crosby and his co-stars, director Frank Tuttle injected *Two for Tonight* with the sugary, romantic silliness that had spoiled a number of Crosby's other musicals. Therefore, *Two for Tonight* emerges as an occasionally funny but generally sporadic and ill-balanced film.

It also tries to cram too many plot devices into its sixty-one minutes. Instead of limiting its focus to one major plot device, *Two for Tonight* spins off in all directions and suffers badly from an unneeded and bothersome romantic subplot revolving around Crosby and the lovely Joan Bennett. Consequently, the film is remembered today primarily as one of Bing Crosby's weakest and most confused screen vehicles, not rescued even by Bing's always pleasant vocalizing.

With Jack Mulhall

With Mary Boland and Charles E. Arnt

With Ethel Merman, Charlie Ruggles and Grace Bradley

Anything Goes
1936

CAST

Billy Crocker (BING CROSBY); Reno Sweeney (ETHEL MERMAN); Reverend Moon (CHARLES RUGGLES); Hope Harcourt (*Ida Lupino*); Oakleigh (*Arthur Treacher*); Bonnie (*Grace Bradley*); Elisha J. Witney (*Robert McWade*); Mrs. Wentworth (*Margaret Dumont*); Bishop Dobson (*Richard Carle*); Captain (*Matt Moore*); Detective (*Ed Gargan*).

CREDITS

A Paramount Picture. Directed by Lewis Milestone. Produced by Benjamin Glazer. Director of Photography: Karl Struss, A.S.C. Art Direction: Hans Dreier and Ernst Fegte. Set Decoration: A. E. Freudeman. Film Editor: Eda Warren. Sound Recording by Jack Goodrich and Don Johnson. Songs by Cole Porter. Additional Songs by Leo Robin, Richard A. Whiting, Hoagy Carmichael, Frederick Hollander, and Edward Heyman. From the Play by Howard Lindsay and Russel Crouse.

SONGS

"You're the Top"
"Anything Goes"
"All Through the Night"
"Blow, Gabriel, Blow"
"I Get a Kick Out of You"
"There'll Always Be a Lady Fair"

Running Time: 92 minutes

With Ethel Merman

A mildly enjoyable but unsatisfying screen version of Cole Porter's 1934 stage hit, *Anything Goes* puts Bing Crosby in hot pursuit of a beautiful but elusive blonde, Hope Harcourt (Ida Lupino). The girl's elusive behavior causes Bing to surmise that she is in trouble, and when he sees her being forced to board a luxury liner, apparently against her will, he decides to follow.

Aboard ship, Bing discovers that the girl is really an English heiress who ran away from home and is now being returned to her family by a stuffy English gentleman, Sir Evelyn Oakleigh (Arthur Treacher). Bing begins to woo the young lady and is pleased when she welcomes his attentions. Bing is less than pleased, however, when he discovers that his boss is on the ship and wouldn't like it if he were to discover Crosby neglecting his job to woo a lovely young lady.

Desperate, Bing masquerades as the gangster accomplice of the Reverend Dr. Moon (Charlie Ruggles), who is really "Moonface Martin," Public Enemy Number Thirteen. Bing successfully eludes his boss, but he discovers that Hope has decided not to see him any more because she thinks he is really a gangster.

Several days later, the boat docks in England and Bing follows Hope through the streets of London in a desperate attempt to square himself with her. The film's closing moments find Bing and Hope smooching in the back seat of a London taxi during a mild rainstorm.

The film moves swiftly, and the staging of "I Get a Kick Out of You" is impressive. However, stage musicals tend to lose a great deal of their original appeal once they are transferred to the screen, and unfortunately, *Anything Goes* is no exception.

Although the Cole Porter songs are delivered with a fair degree of sincerity by Bing Crosby and Ethel Merman, *Anything Goes* lacks the freewheeling spirit that had made the play such a solid hit on the New York state.

For Bing Crosby, this was yet another film in which the performer was required to do little more than be his own pleasant, easygoing self.

With Ida Lupino

Rhythm on the Range
1936

CAST

Jeff Larrabee (BING CROSBY); Doris Halliday (FRANCES FARMER); Buck (BOB BURNS); Emma (*Martha* RAYE); Robert Halliday (*Samuel S. Hinds*); Penelope (*Lucille Gleason*); Shorty (*George E. Stone*); Wabash (*James Burke*); Gila (*Clem Bevans*); Mischa (*Leonid Kinskey*); Clerk (*Emmett Vogan*); Officer (*Duke York*); Conductor (*James Blaine*); Brakeman (*Herbert Ashley*); Porter (*James Thompson*).

CREDITS

A Paramount Picture. Directed by Norman Taurog. Produced by Benjamin Glazer. Screenplay by Walter DeLeon, Sidney Salkow, John C. Moffett, and Francis Martin. Based on a Story by Mervin J. Houser. Director of Photography: Karl Struss, A.S.C. Art Direction: Hans Dreier and Robert Usher. Set Decoration: A. E. Fruedeman. Sound Recording by Gene Merritt and Don Johnson. Musical Direction by Boris Morros. Film Editor: Ellsworth Hoagland. Costumes by Edith Head. Songs by Johnny Mercer, Richard Whiting, Leo Robin, Frederick Hollander, Sam Coslow, Ralph Rainger, Gertrude Ross, Bager Clark, Walter Bullock, Billy Hill, and J. Keirn Brennan.

With Frances Farmer

SONGS

"Empty Saddles"
"Memories"
"Rhythm on the Range"
"Drink It Down"
"I Can't Escape From You"
"I'm an Old Cowhand"
"Mr. Paganini"

Running Time: 85 minutes

During his forty-year career in motion pictures, Bing Crosby starred in only two Westerns, *Rhythm on the Range,* in 1936, and the remake of John Ford's 1939 classic, *Stagecoach,* in 1966. The latter was an admittedly disastrous and overblown remake, but it allowed Crosby to shine in his difficult role. The first Bing Crosby Western, *Rhythm on the Range,* was a well-done musical panorama of life and love on a Western dude ranch, but it offered Crosby no real acting challenge.

Rhythm on the Range cast Crosby in the Gene Autry–style role of a singing cowpoke named Jeff Larrabee who runs an exclusive dude ranch in Southern California with the help of his addle-headed but amiable partner, Buck Burns (Bob Burns). As the film opens, Jeff and Buck are preparing to return to their ranch after winning the grand prize at a high-class New York rodeo. Their prize is a two-thousand-pound champion bull named Cuddles. Jeff decides to take the prize home via freight train and instructs Buck to go ahead to the ranch by himself.

After Buck departs, Jeff and Cuddles board a local freight and are soon on their way back to California. No sooner does the train leave the station, however, than Jeff discovers that he and Cuddles are not the only occupants of the freight car. Behind a wooden crate, Jeff finds a stunningly beautiful young woman (Frances Farmer) wearing sumptuous furs and jewelry. Naturally curious, Jeff asks the girl who she is and how she got there. The girl replies that her name is Doris Halliday and that she hopped the freight to avoid marrying a man she didn't love in New York. She doesn't know anyone in California and has nowhere to stay once she arrives. Jeff invites her to spend a few days as a guest at his ranch.

Arriving in California, Jeff and Doris are greeted at the station by Jeff's partner, Buck. Buck has fallen in love with a daffy young society woman named Emma (Martha Raye) and plans to marry her as soon as he and his new girlfriend can buy a marriage license and find a preacher. Buck explains that Emma is so much in love with him that she is willing to give up her place in society to become Mrs. Buck Burns. In addition, Emma has promised to become a full-fledged cowgirl.

Several weeks later, Jeff and his ranch hands hold an elaborate celebration in honor of Buck and Emma's engagement. During the festivities, Doris takes Jeff aside and confesses that she has fallen in love with him and his simple, honest way of life. Jeff promptly proposes marriage to her, and she eagerly accepts. Before the party is over, Jeff informs all his friends that Buck and Emma aren't the only couple heading for the altar.

Rhythm on the Range is one of the few films in which Bing Crosby was almost completely overshadowed by one of his co-stars. Of course, this was not due to any flaw in his performance; his easy-does-it crooning was simply no match for the side-splitting antics of his twenty-seven-year-old co-worker Martha Raye. Making her motion picture debut in *Rhythm on the Range,* the wacky comedienne utterly stole the film with her hilarious portrayal of the loudmouthed, scatterbrained society dame who falls in love with slow-witted but affable rodeo star Bob Burns. She subsequently finds herself in all kinds of humorous situations while trying desperately to conform to the rough-and-tumble life-style of her cowboy sweetheart. Whether she is shown twirling a lariat or singing "If You Can't Sing It You'll Have to Swing It," Raye is at her absolute best throughout, emerging as the brightest element in a slick and entertaining musical Western.

With Frances Farmer

Pennies From Heaven

1936

CAST

Larry (BING CROSBY); Susan (MADGE EVANS); Patsy (*Edith* FELLOWS); *Gramps* (*Donald* MEEK); Henry (*Louis* ARMSTRONG); Hart (*John Gallaudet*); Crowbar (*Tom Dugan*); Miss Howard (*Nana Bryant*); Warden (*Charles Wilson*); Carmichael (*William Stack*); Briggs (*Tom Ricketts*).

CREDITS

A Columbia Picture. Directed by Norman Z. Mc-Leod. Produced by Emmanuel Cohen. Screenplay by Jo Swerling. Based on *The Peacock's Feather,* by Katherine Leslie Moore. Director of Photography: Robert Pittack. Sound Recording: Glen Rominger. Musical Arrangements by John Scott Trotter. Songs by Arthur Johnson and John Burke.

SONGS

"One, Two, Button My Shoe"
"So Do I"
"Skeleton in the Closet"
"Pennies From Heaven"
"Let's Call a Heart a Heart"
"Now I've Got Some Dreaming to Do"
"What This Country Needs."

Running Time: 80 minutes

Tepid entertainment, rescued from total oblivion only by the perpetual revivals of its ever-popular title song, *Pennies from Heaven* casts Bing Crosby as a wandering troubadour who is sent to prison on a false charge of smuggling. During his term in the

big house, Bing is given a note by a convicted murderer on his way to the electric chair. On the note are the name and address of a small impoverished family currently searching for a permanent home in New Jersey. The prisoner goes on to say that these

With William Stack, Nana Bryant, Stanley Blystone, Stanley Andrews, Edith Fellows and Madge Evans

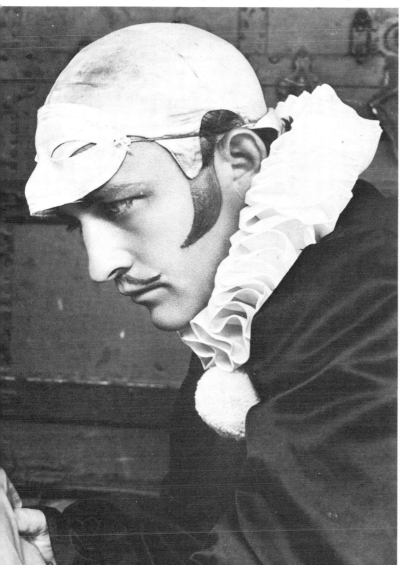

people are the only living relatives of the man he killed and that he would appreciate it if Crosby would look in on them once he is released from jail.

Upon leaving prison, Bing goes to see the family and finds them flat broke and in desperate need of help. Bing informs the family that the last request of the man who killed their relative was that they should inherit a large country estate that once belonged to the killer's family. The family agrees to move into the old estate.

Once they arrive at the old mansion, however, the family begins to have second thoughts when they discover it to be a rather ghoulish old abode that looks as though it could very easily be haunted. This does not worry Bing, however; he comes up with the brilliant idea of turning the old place into a profitable roadside restaurant called the Haunted House Café.

As the singing vagabond, Bing Crosby labors hard in a valiant attempt to establish a believable characterization. In spite of the limitations of the film's ridiculous script, Crosby is successful in presenting his character as a delightfully unorthodox man who scorns the dreary workaday world and is more than content to make his modest living by singing for his supper. However, Bing's first-rate performance is sadly wasted on a totally ineffectual motion picture.

With Edith Fellows   81

With Shirley Ross, Martha Raye and Bob Burns

With Henry Roquemore and Shirley Ross

Waikiki Wedding

1937

CAST

Tony Marvin (BING CROSBY); Shad Buggle (BOB BURNS); Georgia Smith (SHIRLEY ROSS); Myrtle Finch (MARTHA RAYE); J. P. Todhunter (*George Barbier*); Everett Todhunter (*Grady Sutton*); Victor (*Leif Erickson*); Uncle Herman (*Granville Bates*); Kimo (*Anthony Quinn*); Koalani (*Mitchell Lewis*); Muamua (*George Regas*); Priest (*Prince Leilani*); Assistant Purser (*Nick Lukats*); Kaiaka (*Maurice Liu*); Mahina (*Raquel Echeverria*); Dancer (*Miri Rei*); Frame (*Spencer Charters*); Harrison (*Alexander Leftwich*).

CREDITS

A Paramount Picture. Directed by Frank Tuttle. Produced by Arthur Hornblow, Jr. Screenplay by Frank Butler, Don Hartman, Walter DeLeon, and Francis Martin. Based on a Story by Frank Butler and Don Hartman. Director of Photography: Karl Struss, A.S.C. Set Decoration: A.E. Freudeman. Musical Director: Boris Morros. Orchestrations by Victor Young. Arrangements by Al Siegel and Arthur Franklin. Dance Direction by LeRoy Prinz. Film Editor: Paul Weatherwax. Hawaiian Lyrics by Jimmy Lovell. Costumes by Edith Head. Hawaiian Exteriors by Robert C. Bruce. Sound Recording by Gene Merritt and Louis Mesenkop. Song: "Sweet Leilani" by Harry Owens. Other Songs by Ralph Rainger and Leo Robin.

With Martha Raye and Shirley Ross

SONGS
"Sweet Leilani"
"Blue Hawaii"
"In a Little Hula Heaven"
"Sweet Is the Word for You"

Running Time: 89 minutes

With Bob Burns

With Shirley Ross

Waikiki Wedding finds lovely Shirley Ross appearing as a "Pineapple Princess" for a large pineapple concern. She takes part in a publicity scheme on Hawaii and becomes involved with resourceful advertising whiz Bing Crosby.

Similar to the successful *Rhythm on the Range* in both its plot and the principal members of its cast, *Waikiki Wedding* is another mildly enjoyable comedy that enables Crosby to display his talents as a light comedian. As in *Rhythm on the Range*, Crosby is featured opposite a beautiful and talented actress (Shirley Ross), and he is again supported by the comic expertise of two of Hollywood's most durable clowns, Bob Burns and Martha Raye. The latter is particularly delightful throughout the film and very nearly succeeds in once again stealing the show.

In addition to Miss Raye's hilarious shenanigans, *Waikiki Wedding* boasts one of the most believable studio recreations of Hawaii ever filmed, sustaining an exotic Hawaiian atmosphere that very few motion pictures have ever equaled. The film owes much of its authentic atmosphere to Paramount veteran A. E. Freudeman's tasteful set decoration and to Robert C. Bruce's marvelous Hawaiian exteriors. But the greater portion of the picture's convincing tropical aura is provided by the flavorful songs of Harry Owens, Ralph Rainger, and Leo Robin. Some of the more famous tunes include "Sweet Leilani," "In a Little Hula Heaven," and the beautiful "Blue Hawaii."

Although all the musical numbers are delivered in an entertaining manner, the true musical highlight is unquestionably Bing Crosby's mellow rendition of Harry Owen's popular and romantic "Sweet Leilani." Crooning this well-known "Hawaiian" love song as only he could, Crosby provides further proof that he is without peer at delivering light, sentimental ballads, reminding the viewer that he had an incredible vocal range.

Double or Nothing

1937

CAST

Lefty Boylan (BING CROSBY); Liza Lou Lane (MARTHA RAYE); Half Pint (*Andy* DEVINE); Vicki Clark (*Mary* CARLISLE); Pederson (*William Frawley*); Sailor (*Benny Baker*); Jonathan Clark (*Samuel S. Hinds*); Egbert (*William Henry*); Martha Clark (*Fay Holden*); Mr. Dobson (*Walter Kingsford*); Mr. Mitchell (*Gilbert Emery*); Rutherford (*John Gallaudet*).

CREDITS

A Paramount Picture. Directed by Theodore Reed. Produced by Benjamin Glazer. Screenplay by Charles Lederer, Edwin Gelsey, Duke Atterberry, and John C. Moffitt. Based on a Story by M. Coates Webster. Director of Photography: Karl Struss, A.S.C. Film Editor: Edward Dmytryk. Musical Director: Boris Morros. Songs by: John Burke, Sam Coslow, Arthur Johnston, Ralph Freed, Al Siegel, and Burton Lane. Vocal Arrangements: Max Terr and Victor Young. Vocal Supervision by Al Siegel. Musical Adviser: Arthur Franklin.

SONGS

"After You"
"Smarty"
"It's the Natural Thing to Do"
"All You Want to Do Is Dance"
"The Moon Got in My Eyes"

Running Time: 95 minutes

With Mary Carlisle

With Francis Faye, Martha Raye and Harry Barris

Double or Nothing is a flyweight yet interesting entertainment. This cute little musical tale tells of how four down-and-out people are each given the opportunity to inherit one-million dollars from the will of an eccentric philanthropist. Compared with *If I Had a Million*, the earlier Paramount screen study of the sometimes humorous effects of philanthropy, *Double or Nothing* cannot approach the classic status of the earlier film. Still, it is a mildly amusing picture, helped enormously by the marvelous rapport of its four principals—Bing Crosby, Martha Raye, Andy Devine, and William Frawley as the people who find themselves in friendly competition for the legacy.

Each of these performers contributed immensely to the quality of this modest farce and helped to make *Double or Nothing* one of the most successful light comedies released in 1937. Although the film doesn't measure up to *Rhythm on the Range*, it is nonetheless a superb example of the kind of film Bing Crosby became famous for during the 1930s. It is also a definitive illustration of how a film can get by with very little plot as long as it contains a couple of good songs and Bing Crosby sings them.

With William Frawley, Andy Devine and Martha Raye

Doctor Rhythm

1938

CAST

Dr. Bill Remsen (BING CROSBY); Lorelei Dodge-Blodgett (BEATRICE LILLIE); Judy Marlowe (*Mary Carlisle*); Officer O'Roon (*Andy* DEVINE); Al (*Rufe Davis*); Mrs. Twombling (*Laura Hope Crews*); Chris LeRoy (*Fred Keating*); Inspector Bryce (*John Hamilton*); Luke (*Sterling Holloway*); Otis Eaton (*Henry Wadsworth*); Mr. Stenchfield (*Franklin Pangborn*); Mr. Martingale (*William Austin*); Sergeant Olson (*Emory Parnell*); Captain (*Harry Stubbs*); Butler (*Frank Elliot*); Henchman (*Allen Matthews*); Nurse (*Dolores Casey*); Entertainer (*Louis Armstrong*).

CREDITS

A Paramount Picture. Directed by Frank Tuttle. Produced by Emmanuel Cohen. Adaptation by Jo Swerling and Richard Connell. Based on O. Henry's "The Badge of Policeman O'Roon." Director of Photography: Charles Lang, A.S.C. Associate Producer: Herbert Polesie. Assistant Director: Russell Matthews. Additional Comedy Scenes by Dion Titheradge. Musical Director: George Stoll. Orchestrations by John Scott Trotter. Dance Director: Jack Crosby. Songs by Johnny Burke and James V. Monaco.

With Beatrice Lillie

SONGS

"My Heart Is Taking Lessons"
"This Is My Night to Dream"
"On the Sentimental Side"
"Doctor Rhythm"
"Only a Gypsy Knows"
"Trumpet Player's Lament"

Running Time: 80 minutes

With Mary Carlisle

One of Bing Crosby's weakest motion pictures, *Doctor Rhythm* is based on the O. Henry yarn "The Badge of Policeman O' Roon" but is a dull and contrived musical comedy with only a vague resemblance to the short story. Containing perhaps the thinnest story line Crosby was ever forced to muddle through, the film simply presents the performer as an easygoing doctor who replaces his pal Officer Andy Devine as lovely Mary Carlisle's police protector. Of course, before the final fadeout, he also finds himself falling in love with the beautiful Miss Carlisle.

Doctor Rhythm has no remarkable songs to offer, and its threadbare plot is almost too flimsy even to bother about. The film exhibits no real balance or pacing. Several potentially good comedy scenes involving Beatrice Lillie and Andy Devine are sadly negated by the picture's overall lack of any credibility or entertainment value. This is a surprise, considering that *Doctor Rhythm* had an impressive cast of superb comic actors and was directed by the capable Frank Tuttle.

Of course, there are numerous reasons for *Doctor Rhythm*'s unfortunate failure, but one cannot help wondering why Paramount refrained from filming *Doctor Rhythm* as a straight adaptation of the O. Henry classic and decided to transform a viable story property into an uneven and confusing musical. Perhaps the studio was a bit apprehensive about how the moviegoing public would react to seeing musical-comedy stars Bing Crosby and Mary Carlisle in a nonmusical film. But even if this was the case, Paramount should have taken the time and effort to invest the film with a better collection of songs instead of forcing Crosby to make the most of such forgettable numbers as "My Heart Is Taking Lessons" and "This Is My Night to Dream."

With Mary Carlisle

With Donald O'Connor and Fred MacMurray

With Ellen Drew

With Donald O'Connor and Fred MacMurray

Sing You Sinners
1938

CAST

Joe Beebe (BING CROSBY); David Beebe (FRED MAC-MURRAY); Mike Beebe (*Donald O'Connor*); Mother Beebe (*Elizabeth Patterson*); Martha (*Ellen Drew*); Harry Ringmer (*John Gallaudet*); Pete (*William Haade*); Filter (*Paul White*); Boring Lecturer (*Irving Bacon*); Racing Fan (*Tom Dugan*); Nightclub Manager (*Herbert Corthell*).

CREDITS

A Paramount Picture. Produced and Directed by Wesley Ruggles. Original Story and Screenplay by Claude Binyon. Director of Photography: Karl Struss, A.S.C. Art Direction: Hans Dreier and Ernst Fegte. Set Decoration: A. E. Freudeman. Film Editor: Alma Macrorie. Sound Recording by Earl Hayman. Musical Director: Boris Morros. Vocal Arrangements: Max Terr. Assistant Director: Arthur Jacobson. Song: "Small Fry" by Frank Loesser and Hoagy Carmichael. Other Songs by Johnny Burke and James V. Monaco.

SONGS

"Small Fry"
"I've Got a Pocketful of Dreams"
"Laugh and Call it Love"
"Don't Let the Moon Get Away"
"Where Is Central Park?"

Running Time: 88 minutes

With Fred MacMurray, Ellen Drew, Elizabeth Patterson and Donald O'Connor

By 1938, Crosby had established himself as one of the most popular and durable light leading men in motion pictures. His musicals and light comedies had all been enormously successful at the box office, and his status as one of the screen's most likable personalities was generally acknowledged. But whether Crosby could successfully handle a serious dramatic role had yet to be resolved.

For this reason, *Sing You Sinners* rates an extremely important place in Crosby's film career. A seriocomic contemporary drama concerning the exploits of a shiftless young gambler and his patient, loving family, it was the very film to offer Crosby a screen role of pith and substance, in which he could demonstrate his ability as a dramatic actor. Most of his previous screen roles had been limited to portraying charming, romantic, and carefree crooners, always involved with either abandoned children, runaway blondes, villainous gangsters, or homeless old people. This type of role admittedly fit Bing Crosby like an old glove, but it never allowed him to show the true depth of his talent.

Crosby possessed a natural acting skill that could be easily applied to virtually any kind of screen role. This skill would eventually blossom during the forties and fifties but it had remained sadly neglected in his films before *Sing You Sinners,* possibly because the studio was reluctant to cast Crosby in a role that might alter his popular image as the screen's favorite crooner.

The film featured Crosby as Joe Beebe, a happy-go-lucky ne'er-do-well who, at thirty-five, still harbors dreams of the fast buck and is unable to sustain an honest job. His brother Dave (Fred MacMurray) is just the opposite. He is a tough, hardworking garage mechanic who aspires to ownership of his own repair shop. As a result of their opposing views of life, the two are in almost perpetual conflict, much to the dismay of their mother (Elizabeth Patterson) and younger brother Mike (Donald O'Connor).

Despite the family's domestic difficulties, they share one common bond, an intense devotion to music. All three brothers are revealed to be proficient musicians, able to supplement the family income by performing in a local nightspot. But even this profitable diversion soon proves unsatisfactory for the restless Joe. He decides to pack up and head for Los Angeles in the hope of securing a job that yields a more substantial income. Before he leaves, he promises the family that he will make good and that he will send for them as soon as he is settled.

One month later, Mother Beebe receives an encouraging letter from Joe, telling her of his burgeoning business in the second-hand trade. Believing that her eldest son has finally found his place in the world, she sells the house, packs her belongings, and boards the first train to Los Angeles. Once there, however, she discovers that Joe had sold his business after two weeks, to buy a flashy but relatively unknown race horse named Uncle Gus. Furthermore, as a result of this foolish purchase, Joe has been unable to pay his monthly rent and is soon to be evicted.

Although Mother Beebe becomes perturbed at her son's shameful irresponsibility, Joe assures her that Uncle Gus will reap tremendous profits once he is properly trained and groomed. This will take several months, and Joe has but two weeks before his eviction notice is to be served.

One week later, Dave and his fiancée, Martha (Ellen Drew), pay the family an unexpected visit. Dave finds out about Uncle Gus and chastises his brother for being such an irresponsible fool. However, when Derby day arrives, Dave watches in wide-eyed amazement as his brother's horse spectacularly demolishes all the other competitors.

Crosby took full advantage of his first opportunity to enact a screen role of dimension and depth. His Joe Beebe is a deceptively complex man, seeming contented and carefree on the surface but frequently given to moments of introspective despair and self-doubt. It is a skillful characterization, revealing for the first time the more serious side of Bing's talent.

Paris Honeymoon

1939

CAST

Lucky Lawton (BING CROSBY); Manya (FRANCISKA GAAL); Countess De Remi (SHIRLEY ROSS); Peter Karloca (*Akim* TAMIROFF); Ernest (*Edward Everett Horton*); Sitska (*Ben Blue*); Fluschotska (*Rafaela Ottiano*); Count De Remi (*Gregory Gaye*); Pulka (*Alex Melesh*); Huskins (*Raymond Hatton*); Butler (*Keith Kenneth*); Judge (*Michael Visaroff*); The Ancient (*Victor Kilian*).

CREDITS

A Paramount Picture. Directed by Frank Tuttle. Produced by Harlan Thompson. Screenplay by Frank Butler and Don Hartman. Based on a Story by Angela Sherwood. Director of Photography: Karl Struss, A.S.C. Art Direction: Hans Dreier and Ernst Fegte. Set Decoration: A. E. Freudeman. Film Editor: Alma Macrorie. Songs by Leo Robin and Ralph Rainger.

SONGS

"I Have Eyes"
"Sweet Little Headache"
"Funny Old Hills"
"Joobalai"
"The Maiden by the Brook"
"Work While You May"

Running Time: 92 minutes

With Edward Everett Horton

With Gregory Gaye and Shirley Ross

Paris Honeymoon is an attractive comedy. A novel and amusing film that tells the story of an amiable Texas millionaire and his love affair with a beautiful European peasant girl, its dialogue is sharp and brisk and its scenario allows its supporting cast to shine in a rich variety of colorful character roles. Yet this cozy little farce was largely ignored by audiences and underated by critics. One can only hazard a guess why such an entertaining production received such critical lambast, the most practical reason seems to be that *Paris Honeymoon* had the misfortune to be released by Paramount only five months after Bing Crosby's best film to that date, *Sing You Sinners*. As a result, audiences and critics found themselves comparing *Paris Honeymoon* with the earlier film, and most of them were disappointed.

Nevertheless the film is an enjoyable Crosby vehicle. *Paris Honeymoon* features the Groaner in the role of Lucky Lawton, a wealthy Texas tycoon who ventures to Europe to be closer to the equally wealthy lady in his life, Countess De Remi (Shirley Ross). Along the way, however, Lucky and his valet, Ernest (Edward Everett Horton), arrive at a beautiful, rustic mountain village and decide to spend a few months at a spacious Old World castle deep in the mountains.

After one amusing sequence during which Lucky tries to haunt his own castle, the easygoing million-aire meets a beautiful peasant girl (Franciska Gaal) and loses his heart to her. Not surprisingly, Lucky soon discovers that he likes the simple peasant maiden much more than the spoiled countess.

Bing Crosby and Shirley Ross clearly enjoyed their roles in this modest situation comedy. They had worked together in *Waikiki Wedding*, and their experience as a screen team shows through in their scenes together. *Paris Honeymoon* also contained a deft comic performance by Akim Tamiroff in the role of a buffoonish European peasant who runs a rustic pub in the village. Usually cast as a villain, Tamiroff proved with his performance in *Paris Honeymoon* that he was an actor of range and versatility.

But no matter how good all of the actors were, the real stars were the film's truly impressive scenic designs, most notably the quaint mountain village and the castle that Crosby and his valet rent. The latter was a particularly elaborate and convincing set featuring a huge drawing room, winding staircases, and large pillars. In fact, the castle set could probably give the set from any Gothic horror film an honest run for its money. The castle's overall weirdness lends itself beautifully to the scene in which Bing tries to haunt the place by floating around the castle's dank chambers as a disembodied head, singing "I Ain't Got No Body."

With Franciska Gaal and Shirley Ross

With Joan Blondell

With Joan Blondell, Mischa Auer and Robert Kent

East Side of Heaven
1939

CAST

Denny Martin (BING CROSBY); Mary Wilson (JOAN BLONDELL); Mona Barrett (*Irene* HERVEY); Nicky (*Mischa* AUER); Cyrus Barrett, Sr. (*C. Aubrey* SMITH); Claudius De Wolfe (*Jerome* COWAN); The Baby (*"Sandy"*); Cyrus Barrett, Jr. (*Robert Kent*); Mrs. Travers (*Mary Carr*); Fisher (*Douglas Wood*); Loftus (*Arthur Hoyt*); Hinkle (*Russell Hicks*); Bobby (*Jackie Gerlich*); Henry Smith (*Edward Earle*); Mrs. Smith (*Dorothy Christy*); Mrs. Kelly (*Jane Jones*); Doorman (*J. Farrell MacDonald*).

CREDITS

A Universal Picture. Directed by David Butler. Original Story by David Butler and Herbert Polesie. Screenplay by William Conselman. Director of Photography: George Robinson, A.S.C. Art Direction: Jack Otterson. Set Decoration: Russell A. Gausman. Sound Recording: Bernard B. Brown. Assistant Director: Joseph A. McDonough. Songs by James V. Monaco and Johnny Burke.

SONGS

"Sing a Song of Moonbeams"
"That Sly Old Gentleman"
"East Side of Heaven"
"Hang Your Heart on a Hickory Limb"
"Rings on My Fingers"
"Ida"

Running Time: 85 minutes

With Mischa Auer

With Mischa Auer and "Baby Sandy" Henville

A generally good but unremarkable vehicle, *East Side of Heaven* is similar to Crosby's earlier *Pennies from Heaven*, featuring the Bingle as a man who suddenly finds himself acting as the father by proxy for an endearing child. This time, Bing is cast as an easygoing fellow who becomes the imitation papa for a ten-month-old baby named Sandy and finds himself getting involved with the child's turbulent family. Since the baby's family insists upon coming to blows over who should be the child's guardian, there are a great many custody squabbles before the final happy reconciliation that satisfies everyone.

Even though it is a completely innocuous enter-

tainment, *East Side of Heaven* is one of Crosby's better films away from Paramount. His performance is noteworthy for good acting, particularly when he is given the opportunity to establish his rather one-sided rapport with the infant. These scenes allowed Crosby to display a sensitivity that is really quite touching.

To the film's credit, *East Side of Heaven* has more than its share of good comedy scenes in which veteran performers like Mischa Auer, C. Aubrey Smith, and Joan Blondell are shown off to best advantage.

The Star Maker

1939

CAST

Larry Earl (BING CROSBY); Jane Gray (*Linda Ware*); Mary (*Louise* CAMPBELL); "Speed" King (*Ned Sparks*); Carlotta Salvini (*Laura Hope Crews*); Himself (*Walter Damrosch*); Stella (*Janet Waldo*); Mr. Proctor (*Thurston Hall*); Steel Worker (*Billy Gilbert*).

CREDITS

A Paramount Picture. Directed by Roy Del Ruth. Produced by Charles R. Rogers. Screenplay by Frank Butler, Don Hartman, and Art Caesar. Based upon a Story by Art Caesar and William Pierce. Suggested by the Career of Gus Edwards. Director of Photography: Karl Struss, A.S.C. Art Direction: Hans Dreier and Robert Usher. Set Decoration: A. E. Freudeman. Film Editor: Alma Macrorie. Sound Recording by Charles Hisserich and Richard Olsen. Musical Direction: Alfred Newman. Costumes by Edith Head. New Songs by Johnny Burke and James V. Monaco.

SONGS

"An Apple for the Teacher"
"Go Fly a Kite"
"A Man and His Dream"
"Still the Bluebird Sings"

Running Time: 94 minutes

With Linda Ware

With Darryl Hickman (dancing)

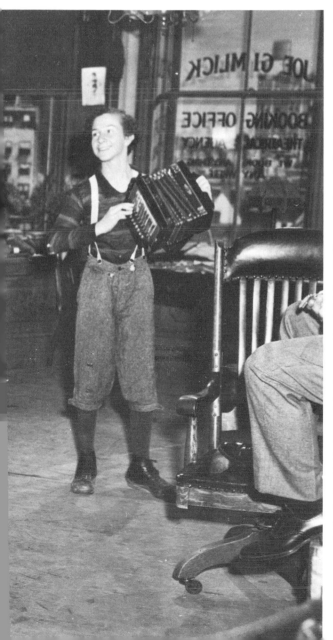

Contrary to popular belief, *The Star Maker* is not really a biography of pioneer showman Gus Edwards; it is a half-hearted and uneven musical, only loosely based on the life and career of the vaudeville impresario. The film is merely the contrived story of an ambitious young songwriter whose show-business career is only partly reminiscent of that of Edwards.

The film opens as an unsuccessful young singer-songwriter named Larry Earl (Crosby) decides to chuck his show-business ambitions and settle down with his fiancée, Mary (Louise Campbell). Married and with definite responsibilities, Larry is forced to take a monotonous job as a floor walker in a department store. This soon proves unrewarding for the talented young fellow, and he begins to feel the show-business urge once again.

Deciding that show business is his true calling, Larry begins to think seriously about forming his own vaudeville troupe. Larry also wisely surmises that if his act is to be successful, it must be unique. With this in mind, Larry decides to form a song-and-dance group comprised of children under seventeen.

Larry hires six grubby neighborhood newsboys, and surprisingly, within a few weeks he transforms them into a first-rate vaudeville ensemble. The group's ability, coupled with its performers' youth, prompts a big-time theater owner (Thurston Hall) to give Larry and his kids a spot in an upcoming musical revue.

Opening night is an enormous triumph for Larry and his troupe, and within a few months the group becomes the hottest vaudeville act in the business. Larry is soon able to expand his operation, and before long he is touring the country with more than fifty talented child performers. All goes splendidly for Larry until he encounters stiff opposition from the people at the Bureau of Child Welfare, who order Larry to shut his operation down. When he asks why, they inform him that there is a law strictly forbidding anyone from making a child work after eight in the evening.

With Dorothy Vaughan and Bodil Rosing

Although Larry considers the law unfair and foolish, he finds that he has no choice but to obey. He dismisses all his performers and begins to look for a new avenue of show business for his talents as an innovative showman.

After months of searching, Larry finally hits upon the idea of going into another totally new facet of entertainment, radio.

Containing too many songs and too little plot, *The Star Maker* is a sterling example of an interest-ing idea that turned sour when brought to the screen. One can only speculate about how the film would have turned out if presented as a true biogra-phy of Gus Edwards, but since he was the discoverer of such show business personalities as Eddie Cantor, George Jessel, Eleanor Powell, Ray Bolger, Sally Rand, Jack Pearl, and the Lane sisters, it probably would have emerged as a fascinating screen biogra-phy.

Road to Singapore

1940

CAST

Josh Mallon (BING CROSBY); Mima (DOROTHY LA-MOUR); Ace Lannigan (BOB HOPE); Joshua Mallon IV (*Charles Coburn*); Gloria Wycott (*Judith Barrett*); Caesar (*Anthony Quinn*); Achilles Bombanassa (*Jerry Colonna*); Morgan Wycott (*Pierre Watkin*); Gordon Wycott (*Gaylord Pendleton*); Timothy Willow (*Johnny Arthur*); Sir Malcolm Drake (*Miles Mander*); Zato (*Pedro Regas*); Babe (*Greta Granstedt*); Bill (*Ed Gargan*); Sailor (*John Kelly*); Sailor's Wife (*Kitty Kelly*); Native Boy (*Benny Inocencio*); Ninky Poo (*Gloria Franklin*); Dancing Girl (*Carmen D'Antonio*); Secretary (*Harry C. Bradley*).

CREDITS

A Paramount Picture. Directed by Victor Schertzinger. Produced by Harlan Thompson. Screenplay by Don Hartman and Frank Butler. Based upon a Story by Harry Hervey. Director of Photography: William Mellor, A.S.C. Art Direction: Hans Dreier and Robert Odell. Film Editor: Paul Weatherwax. Sound Recording by Earl Hayman and John Cope. Musical Director: Victor Young. Dances Staged by LeRoy Prinz.

SONGS

"Too Romantic"
"Sweet Potato Piper"
"Kaigoon" (by Johnny Burke and James V. Monaco)
"The Moon and the Willow Tree"
"Captain Custard" (by Johnny Burke and Victor Schertzinger)

Running Time: 84 minutes

With Bob Hope

With Judith Barrett

With Dorothy Lamour and Bob Hope

Road to Singapore has the distinction of being the most successful failure in the history of Hollywood. An adventure comedy featuring Bing Crosby and Bob Hope as carefree vagabonds who find themselves vying for the affections of lovely native princess Dorothy Lamour, the film emerged as Paramount's most financially successful production of the year and one of the top moneymaking films of the decade. The film's commercial success gave Paramount the impetus to go ahead with its plan to feature Crosby and Hope in what would eventually become the studio's most famous comedy series.

Road to Singapore is the "black sheep" of the *Road* films and perhaps the weakest of them. It isn't really a bad film; it just isn't anywhere nearly as hilarious or thoroughly entertaining as any of the subsequent entries in the series. The main reason is that *Road to Singapore*'s humor appears tame in comparison to the sheer lunacy of *Road to Zanzibar* and others of the series. Whereas later *Road* films became successful primarily because they featured Crosby and Hope in some of their wackiest and funniest situations, *Road to Singapore* contains practically no outrageous humor and offers little more than an outdated collection of feeble sight gags, corny one-liners, and tired slapstick routines.

The reason for the film's triumph continues to baffle both critics and historians. They cannot figure out why a film that most critics were content to dismiss as mildly amusing but hopelessly uneven should be such an enormous box-office hit.

Crosby is introduced as Josh Mallon, an easy-going, carefree young man whose stern father (Charles Coburn) wants him to take over someday as president of the family's multi-million-dollar shipping corporation. In spite of his dad's wishes, however, Josh has no interest in the shipping business and would much prefer to spend his time bumming around the world with his affable sidekick,

Ace Lannigan (Bob Hope). Despite the continued protests of his father and his lovely fiancée, Gloria (Judith Barrett), Josh insists upon living and acting as he pleases. Before long he and Ace depart for Singapore in the hope of getting as far away from civilization as possible.

At their destination, the boys rent a small bungalow and proceed to explore the colorful nightlife in and around the port of Kaigoon. At one of the more dubious night spots, the boys witness a hazardous vaudeville act in which an attractive young native girl named Mima (Dorothy Lamour) allows a burning cigarette to be snapped out of her mouth by the skilled whiphand of a South American *gaucho* (Anthony Quinn). Fearing for her safety, Josh and Ace abduct the girl and take her back to their modest bungalow.

The young woman thanks the boys for their concern and agrees to pay them back by becoming their full-time housemaid, in exchange for room and board. Naturally, Josh and Ace eagerly agree.

The boys quickly discover that two healthy young men and one luscious young woman cannot live under the same roof without complications. The worst of these is that both Josh and Ace have fallen in love with Mima and soon find themselves competing with each other for her affections. Although Mima appreciates their feelings, she makes it clear that she is attracted to only one of them and that she won't reveal who the lucky fellow is until she is certain of her own true feelings.

A few weeks later, Josh informs Mima that his father and his fiancée have begged him to return to civilization with them. Josh assures Mima that he would comply with their request only if Mima were to tell him that Ace is the one she loves.

Feeling that Josh belongs in America with his father and his fiancée, Mima reluctantly informs him that Ace is the man she truly loves. Although he is disappointed, Josh wishes her every happiness. After congratulating Ace for winning the woman, the deflated Josh reluctantly departs for America.

Sometime later, Josh discovers that Mima was only pretending to be in love with Ace because she did not wish to come between Josh and his fiancée. Upon learning this, Josh boards the first boat back to Singapore to be with the woman he truly loves.

Perhaps *Road to Singapore*'s success can be attributed to the almost magical ability of its two stars to rise above inferior material. As everyone knows, both Crosby and Hope have had to grapple with a number of inadequate scripts, and they became Hollywood's absolute masters at the art of making something out of nothing. *Road to Singapore* is more than likely a case in point. The film could stand as a prime example of how even a third-rate comedy script can be transformed into something successful when entrusted to performers like Hope and Crosby.

If I Had My Way

1940

CAST

Buzz Blackwell (BING CROSBY); Patricia Johnson (GLORIA JEAN); Joe Johnson (*Charles* WINNINGER); Swenson (*El* BRENDEL); Jarvis Johnson (*Allyn Joslyn*); Fred Johnson (*Donald Woods*); Brenda Johnson (*Claire Dodd*); Blair (*Moroni Olsen*); Miss Corbett (*Kathryn Adams*); Marian Johnson (*Nana Bryant*).

CREDITS

A Universal Picture. Produced and Directed by David Butler. Screenplay by William Conselman and James V. Kern. Director of Photography: George Robinson, A.S.C. Art Direction: Jack Otterson. Set Decoration: Russell A. Gausman. Film Editor: Irene Morra. Sound Supervisor: Bernard Brown. Sound Recording: Charles Carroll. Assistant Director: Joseph McDonough. Gowns by Vera West. Songs by Johnny Burke and James V. Monaco.

SONGS

"I Haven't the Time to Be a Millionaire"
"Meet the Sun Halfway"
"If I Had My Way"
"April Played the Fiddle"
"Pessimistic Character"

Running Time: 94 minutes

With Gloria Jean and Charles Winninger

With Gloria Jean and Joe King

One of the lesser items in the Crosby screen career, *If I Had My Way* fails in its attempt to tug at the audience's heart strings. It begins as an amiable construction worker (Crosby) takes charge of the daughter (Gloria Jean) of one of his co-workers who was killed during a hazardous assignment on one of the nation's highest bridges. Learning that the child has relatives in the East, Crosby and his friend Axel (El Brendel) accompany Gloria to New York, hoping to find her great uncle (Charles Winninger). In New York, Bing and Axel find Gloria's Uncle Charles, and the old man welcomes her with open arms. Meanwhile, Axel blows their bankroll buying a small neighborhood restaurant, only to discover that the place is actually nothing more than a worthless flea trap. The resourceful Crosby, however, saves the day when he transforms the place into a high-class nightclub.

If I Had My Way is almost forgotten today, and to see it today makes it easy to see why. Having none of the charm and spirit that make many other Crosby films delightful in spite of their lightweight plots, *If I Had My Way* is an almost embarrassingly dated olio in which the performers are forced to struggle through an incredible maze of tedious musical routines, outmoded comedy bits, and dramatic moments completely saturated with schmaltz. As a result, Crosby and his co-stars are powerless to do much with the film's creaky script. What emerges on screen is ninety-four minutes of extremely uneven entertainment.

The film contains still another of veteran character actor Charles Winninger's portrayals of an old, formerly great vaudeville trouper who shows everyone that he still has what it takes, but one gets the impression that it has all been done before. It is extremely hard to sit through *If I Had My Way* without getting the feeling that one is witnessing a painful rehash of all those "Give My Regards to Broadway"–type films that have sadly outlived their own entertainment value.

Rhythm on the River
1940

CAST

Bob Sommers (BING CROSBY); Cherry Lane (MARY MARTIN); Oliver Courtney (BASIL RATHBONE); Billy Starbuck (*Oscar Levant*); Charlie Goodrich (*Oscar Shaw*); Uncle Caleb (*Charlie Grapewin*); Millie Starling (*Lillian Cornell*); Mr. Westlake (*William Frawley*); Country Cousin (*Jean Cagney*); Mr. Schwartz (*Charles Lane*); Himself (*John Scott Trotter*); Patsy Flick (*Phyllis Kennedy*); Woody (*Wingy Mannone*); Bates (*Brandon Hurst*); Uncle (*Pierre Watkin*); Elevator Boy (*Billy Benedict*).

CREDITS

A Paramount Picture. Directed by Victor Schertzinger. Produced by William Le Baron. Screenplay by Dwight Taylor. Based on a Story by Billy Wilder and Jacques Thery. Director of Photography: Ted Tetzlaff, A.S.C. Art Direction: Hans Dreier and Ernst Fegte. Film Editor: Hugh Bennett. Sound Recording by Earl Hayman and Richard Olsen. Costumes by Edith Head. Music by Victor Young. New Songs by Johnny Burke and James V. Monaco. Orchestrations by John Scott Trotter.

SONGS

"Rhythm on the River"
"Only Forever"
"That's for Me"
"What Would Shakespeare Have Said"
"Ain't It a Shame About Mame?"
"When the Moon Comes Over Madison Square Garden"

Running Time: 92 minutes

With Mary Martin

With Mary Martin

With Wingy Mannone (on trumpet)

Rhythm on the River was not only Crosby's best film since *Sing You Sinners*, but it also marked the major turning point in his career. A bright and entertaining glimpse of the songwriting profession, the film was produced at the beginning of the pinnacle period of Bing's motion-picture career.

Crosby had always enjoyed steady popularity as a movie personality, but not until the decade following this film was he able to establish himself as a superstar. His next nine years at Paramount found Crosby starring in a string of high-quality musicals and semidramatic films so thoroughly polished and well-produced that they made many of his thirties outings seem shallow. As a result, Crosby found his popularity at an all-time high, and during this peak era (from *Rhythm on the River* in 1940 to *A Connecticut Yankee in King Arthur's Court* in 1949) the relaxed and carefree Groaner emerged as one of the most successful screen stars in history.

Rhythm on the River is about the adventures of an extremely talented but hopelessly lazy young songwriter named Bob Sommers (Bing Crosby). Although Bob's talent is such that he could easily make a small fortune composing popular songs, he is basically simple and unambitious, and his greatest dream in life is to own a small catboat. In spite of his lack of ambition, Bob sometimes finds it necessary to earn extra money by ghost writing for a celebrated tunesmith, Oliver Courtney (Basil Rathbone).

Courtney was once a prolific songwriter, but he lost his ability to write music when his wife took a powder with another man. Although Courtney prefers to think of his wife as dead and has even immortalized her in a song entitled "Goodbye to Love," his droll and cynical assistant Billy Starbuck (Oscar Levant) periodically reminds Courtney, "She didn't die; she got fat. She married a guy from Naples who owned a one-armed spaghetti joint." But no matter how often Starbuck tries to jar Courtney out of his dreamworld, the composer still has to rely on ghost writers to sustain his reputation.

Weary of the lucrative but thankless business of ghost writing, Bob and another of Courtney's "ghosts," lovely Cherry Lane (Mary Martin), decide to stop living in Courtney's shadow and try to make it on their own. Although Courtney warns them it will be virtually impossible for two unknowns to get a song published, they are fiercely determined. They begin making the rounds of the New York music publishers.

Courtney's warning soon proves correct, and one of the publishers (William Frawley) tells Bob and Cherry that they'll never get anywhere by imitating a composer as well-known as Oliver Courtney. Caught in a situation for which there is no solution, Cherry takes a job as a nightclub singer and Bob returns to his uncle's farm in the country.

Meanwhile, Courtney begins to get panicky because his inability to create songs is holding up production on a one-hundred-thousand-dollar musical play. Courtney decides to incorporate one of Bob and Cherry's best songs, a beautiful love song called "Only Forever," into the show's libretto. The only trouble is that Bob instructed Courtney never to use the song because it held a very special meaning for Bob and Cherry.

When Bob learns of Courtney's plan, he tries to stop Courtney from presenting "his" newest song to the public. At the last minute, Courtney redeems himself by announcing to the public that the collaborators on his new musical will be a couple of up-and-coming young songwriters named Bob Sommers and Cherry Lane.

Not only is *Rhythm on the River* a brisk and extremely well-written screen comedy, but its photography, music, costumes, and direction are all of the highest caliber. The film's art direction adds further proof that Paramount's Hans Dreier was a master at incorporating scenic designs that tremendously enhanced the mood and flavor of a motion picture. Particularly superb is the stylish dismantled riverboat, the *Arabella,* which Dreier skillfully employs as a haven wherein Bob composes all his best music.

Rhythm on the River also boasts wonderful performances from Crosby, Mary Martin, and particularly Basil Rathbone as the pompous, neurotic, and egotistical Oliver Courtney. Rathbone's hilarious portrayal is a delightful change of pace that allows this peerless movie villain one of his rare displays of the lighter and more amusing side of his talent.

With Joan Marsh

Road to Zanzibar
1941

CAST

Chuck Reardon (BING CROSBY); Fearless Frazier (BOB HOPE); Donna Latour (DOROTHY LAMOUR); Julia (*Una Merkel*); Charles Kimble (*Eric Blore*); Soubrette (*Iris Adrian*); Dimples (*Joan Marsh*); Fat Lady (*Ethel Greer*); Saunders (*Georges Renavent*); Slave Trader (*Douglass Dumbrille*); Proprietor (*Luis Alberni*); Le Bec (*Lionel Royce*); Thonga (*Buck Woods*); Witch Doctor (*Leigh Whipper*); Boy (*Leo Gorcey*); Chief (*Noble Johnson*); Agua (*Charlie Gemora*).

CREDITS

A Paramount Picture. Directed by Victor Schertzinger. Produced by Paul Jones. Based on a Story by Don Hartman and Sy Bartlett. Screenplay by Frank Butler and Don Hartman. Director of Photography: Ted Tetzlaff, A.S.C. Art Direction: Hans Dreier and Robert Usher. Sound Recording by Earl Hayman and Don Johnson. Film Editor: Alma Macrorie. Costumes by Edith Head. Music by Victor Young. Dance Direction: LeRoy Prinz. New Songs by James Van Heusen and Johnny Burke.

SONGS

"You Lucky People You"
"It's Always You"
"You're Dangerous"
"On the Road to Zanzibar"
"Birds of a Feather"

Running Time: 92 minutes

With Bob Hope

With Leo Gorcey

115

With Iris Adrian (left)

Paramount hadn't had much faith in *Road to Singapore*. It was an uninspired comedy vehicle, given over to Crosby and Hope after George Burns and Fred MacMurray had flatly rejected it. It had very little plot, its gags were decidedly unfunny, and its meager collection of songs was nothing to write home about. Yet, to the astonishment of everyone, including the studio, the film became an almost unprecedented Hollywood success.

Not surprisingly, the film's success prompted the studio to build a comedy series around the zany antics of Hope and Crosby. Before long the two were teamed once again with Dorothy Lamour in a second *Road* adventure. But whereas the first film of

the series had been a relatively mild little comic exercise, the second, *Road to Zanzibar,* was a wild, madcap affair in which Hope and Crosby were allowed to ad-lib most of their scenes, break up in front of the camera, and generally raise nearly every other conceivable kind of havoc on the set.

This mischievous behavior undoubtedly chagrined the picture's director, Victor Schertzinger (who reportedly threw up his hands in helpless resignation at one point during the filming), but it made the film a scatterbrained satire of every jungle-adventure epic Hollywood ever made. Although it is certainly not in the same league with some of the later films in the series, *Road to Zanzibar* is an

With Una Merkel and Dorothy Lamour

exceedingly funny motion picture. It was responsible for establishing the wacky plot formula used in the succeeding *Road* adventures.

Road to Zanzibar casts Crosby and Hope as smooth-talking conmen who must flee to an exotic corner of the world to escape the wrath of someone they have swindled. They have sold a phony diamond mine to a dangerous European cut-throat named Le Bec (Lionel Royce), and are forced to beat it for Zanzibar when they discover that Le Bec is out for their blood.

In Zanzibar, they encounter two homeless women (Dorothy Lamour and Una Merkel) who sweet-talk Bob and Bing into financing a full-scale safari across the continent to locate Dorothy's long-lost brother. During the safari, however, the boys discover that the object of the search is not Dorothy's brother, but a wealthy British landowner whom Dorothy plans to marry.

Feeling that they have been taken advantage of, Crosby and Hope decide to abandon the safari and return to Zanzibar. This proves difficult, however, when they discover that Dorothy and Una have abandoned *them* in the jungle, apparently having decided that they no longer need male companionship. This naturally angers Bob and Bing, but their anger soon turns into fear when they find themselves surrounded by a hostile tribe of starving cannibals.

Much to the boys' surprise, the cannibals do not appear to have any intention of eating them. The reason is that the natives believe Hope and Crosby to be a couple of mysterious gods from an unknown land, and they begin to treat the boys like royalty. The tribal witch doctor (Leigh Whipper), however, is not convinced that Bob and Bing are sacred, and he convinces the tribe's chief (Noble Johnson) that Hope and Crosby should be made to prove that they are gods. Deciding to put it to the test, the chief arranges a wrestling match between Bob and a ferocious gorilla named Agua. Needless to say, the gorilla wins.

After "patty-caking" themselves out of the clutches of the natives, Hope and Crosby meet up with Dorothy and Una once again, and all is well before the final fade-out.

Road to Zanzibar allows Bing and Bob each to have his own golden moments of comedy, and it gives Dorothy Lamour the opportunity to portray a woman of wit and sophistication, as opposed to the by-now-stereotyped role of the brooding, sarong-clad native maiden. There are many priceless comedy scenes in the film (such as Crosby and Hope teaching a bunch of cannibals to play patty-cake and, of course, Bob's superlative wrestling match with the not too frightening gorilla, played by veteran Hollywood "ape man" Charlie Gemora). However, perhaps the funniest scene is the delightfully incongruous sight of Bing Crosby lightly crooning the deliberately ridiculous lyrics to "On the Road to Zanzibar" while a chorus of natives chants the completely meaningless phrase "ba-toom-bomba" over and over again.

With Bob Hope

With Mary Martin, Brian Donlevy, and Carolyn Lee

Birth of the Blues

1941

CAST

Jeff Lambert (BING CROSBY); Betty Lou Cobb (MARY MARTIN); Memphis (BRIAN DONLEVY); Aunt Phoebe Cobb (*Carolyn Lee*); Louey (*Eddie "Rochester" Anderson*); Pepper (*Jack Teagarden*); Blackie (*J. Carrol Naish*); Mr. Granet (*Cecil Kellaway*); Limpy (*Warren Hymer*); Wolf (*Horace McMahon*); Ruby (*Ruby Elzy*); Maizie (*Barbara Pepper*); Deek (*Dan Beck*); Suds (*Harry Barris*); Leo (*Perry Botkin*); Piano Player (*Harry Rosenthal*); Skeeter (*Donald Kerr*); Mr. Lambert (*Minor Watson*); Jeff (as a boy) (*Ronnie Cosbey*).

CREDITS

A Paramount Picture. Directed by Victor Schertzinger. Produced by B. G. De Sylva. Screenplay by Harry Tugend and Walter DeLeon. Based on a Story by Harry Tugend. Director of Photography: William Mellor, A.S.C. Art Direction: Hans Dreier and Ernst Fegte. Film Editor: Paul Weatherwax. Sound Recording by Earl Hayman and John Cope. Costumes by Edith Head. Music by Robert Emmett Dolan. Process Photography by Farciot Edouart. Songs by Johnny Mercer, Robert Emmett Dolan, Harry Tugend, W. C. Handy, B. G. DeSylva, Lew Brown, Ray Henderson, Edward Madden and Gus Edwards.

With Mary Martin and Brian Donlevy

SONGS

"The Waiter, the Porter and the Upstairs Maid"
"Gotta Go to the Jailhouse"
"Memphis Blues"
"St. Louis Blues"
"Birth of the Blues"
"By the Light of the Silvery Moon"

Running Time: 85 minutes

Many motion pictures have attempted to capture the flavor and spirit of the fascinating American musical phenomenon known as jazz. Most of these films have been unsuccessful, failing to realize that for a jazz story to be effectively brought to the screen, it must not only contain selections of great jazz, but it must also try to touch upon the private lives and personal struggles of the talented musicians for whom jazz is a way of life. Of course, a handful of Hollywood films accomplished this task (such as Anatole Litvak's *Blues in the Night*, Michael Curtiz's *Young Man with a Horn*, and John Cassavetes' underrated *Too Late Blues*), but one of the most entertaining is Victor Schertzinger's colorful *Birth of the Blues*.

Although it seems on the surface to be nothing more than an above-average musical vehicle for Bing Crosby, Mary Martin, and Brian Donlevy, *Birth of the Blues* is actually a valiant attempt by Hollywood to depict the so-called birth of jazz in a way that almost any filmgoer could appreciate.

The opening of the film deals with the problems of a young lad named Jeff Lambert. Although he is only twelve, Jeff is a remarkably bright boy of extraordinary musical aptitude and ability. Although the boy's father has spent a small fortune to have Jeff taught the fundamentals of classical clarinet, the lad prefers to spend his time with a group of black jazz men who perform in a dive on Bourbon Street. As the boy grows into manhood, his love for jazz intensifies, and he forms his own group, much to the chagrin of his aging father.

Now in his late twenties, Jeff (Crosby) and his boys have been unable to secure a job at any of the classier New Orleans cabarets and have been forced to limit their playing to street corners and to one-night stands in some of the dingier nightclubs. When his lead trombone player asks Jeff why the band can't seem to get anywhere, the young clarinetist replies that he thinks the main problem is that the group lacks a hot trumpet player.

Jeff begins to search throughout New Orleans in the hope of finding a trumpet man who can fill the bill. He finds one in a local jail and promises to bail the fellow out as soon as he can raise the money. This he does, and the trumpet player, a laconic chap named Memphis (Brian Donlevy), agrees to become a member of Jeff's band.

With a great trumpet player, Jeff's band now rises quickly to prominence. They get a job at a posh New Orleans night spot and become the most popular jazz band on Bourbon Street. All goes well until they find out that the owner of the club, Blackie (J. Carrol Naish), is a racketeer who uses his night spot only as a convenient front for his criminal interests.

Jeff and the boys decide to leave Blackie's club and go on to other things. But when they tell Blackie of their plans, the gangster threatens to rub them out one by one. Jeff takes a swing at Blackie, which causes a violent saloon brawl between Blackie and his gang and Jeff and his boys. During the slugfest, Jeff's good friend Louey (Eddie "Rochester" Anderson) is injured when he is cracked over the head with a bottle.

When the riot is over, Jeff and the boys take the unconscious Louey home to his wife, Ruby (Ruby Elzy). As she tearfully bemoans her husband's injury, Jeff and the band play a moving musical tribute to their fallen comrade. This seems to touch the old fellow's spirit, and he slowly, painfully awakens, to tell Jeff and Ruby that he is all right.

A few weeks later, Jeff and his band have still another unpleasant run-in with Blackie. This time, the gangster falls victim to his own evil-doing when he is accidentally killed by one of his own henchmen.

Birth of the Blues is a superb blend of drama, comedy, and music. Crosby is especially fond of this film. It contains flawless performances by Crosby, Mary Martin, and Brian Donlevy as the three principals, and its direction (by veteran comedy director Victor Schertzinger) is delightfully brisk. But the best thing about the film is, of course, its wonderful use of some classic jazz compositions, most notably W. C. Handy's "Saint Louis Blues." This selection is not only used as background music throughout the film, but it is also employed to great effect during the scene in which jazz singer Ruby Elzy laments over her husband's injury. In the highlight of the picture, Miss Elzy renders the torch song while Crosby's faithful band (seen only in shadow) provides the appropriate musical backdrop. It is a vivid and moving sequence in an extremely enjoyable and expertly produced motion picture.

With Brian Donlevy

With Carolyn Lee and Mary Martin

With Marjorie Reynolds

Holiday Inn
1942

CAST

Jim Hardy (BING CROSBY); Ted Hanover (FRED ASTAIRE); Linda Mason (*Marjorie Reynolds*); Lila Dixon (*Virginia Dale*); Danny Reid (*Walter Abel*); Mamie (*Louise Beavers*); Parker (*John Gallaudet*); Dunbar (*James Bell*); Gus (*Irving Bacon*); Vanderbilt (*Shelby Bacon*); Flower Shop Owner (*Leon Belasco*); Bandleader (*Harry Barris*); Cigarette Girl (*Judith Gibson*); Hat-check Girl (*Katharine Booth*).

CREDITS

A Paramount Picture. Produced and Directed by Mark Sandrich. Screenplay by Claude Binyon. Adapted by Elmer Rice from an Original Idea by Irving Berlin. Director of Photography: David Abel. Art Direction: Hans Dreier and Roland Anderson. Sound Recording by Earl Hayman and John Cope. Film Editor: Ellsworth Hoagland. Costumes by Edith Head. Makeup Supervision by Wally Westmore. Musical Director: Robert Emmett Dolan. Dance Director: Danny Dare. Songs by Irving Berlin.

SONGS

"Be Careful, It's My Heart"
"I'll Capture Your Heart"
"Abraham"
"Plenty to Be Thankful For"
"White Christmas"
"Let's Start the New Year Right"
"Happy Holidays"

Running Time: 101 minutes

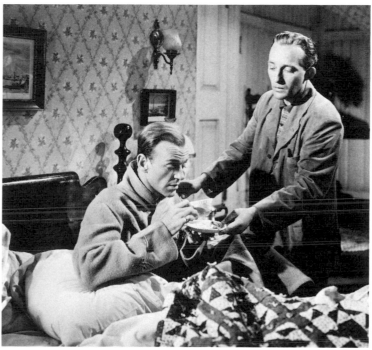

With Fred Astaire

With Virginia Dale

Holiday Inn is perhaps Crosby's most nearly perfect musical, as well as one of the most enjoyable motion pictures produced during the 1940s.

The film's enormous entertainment value and popularity could hardly be attributed to happy accident. Its two leading roles were portrayed by Crosby and Fred Astaire, and Irving Berlin composed the score. *Holiday Inn* was also blessed with an inventive storyline.

Adapted by playwright Elmer Rice from an original idea by Mr. Berlin, *Holiday Inn* tells the charming story of a light-hearted singer who decides to open an exclusive night club in Connecticut that

would be open to the general public only on holidays. This intriguing plotline not only paves the way for some outstanding musical routines, deftly handled by Crosby, Fred Astaire, Marjorie Reynolds, and Virginia Dale, but it also presents veteran musical director Mark Sandrich with an excellent groundwork on which to build an engrossing musical tribute to the different American holidays that never seems the least bit corny. Sandrich's command of the musical cinema is in clear evidence throughout. Sandrich handles the romantic element in the film in a much more believable fashion than most such subplots, providing the stars with the op-

With Virginia Dale and Fred Astaire

With Marjorie Reynolds

With Marjorie Reynolds

portunity to do some straight acting in addition to their song-and-dance routines.

Holiday Inn is not a large-scale musical extravaganza, but actually the intimate story of two affable and talented nightclub entertainers named Jim Hardy (Crosby) and Ted Hanover (Astaire). As the film opens, the easygoing Jim is preparing to quite show business and retire to a small but profitable farm in New England. He explains to Ted that he has grown weary of the backbreaking schedules and long hours of a show-business career, and he wants more leisure time in which to do as he pleases.

Jim soon discovers that the life of a farmer is anything but leisurely, and he soon retires to a rest home to recover from the grind of farming.

After his brief stay in the sanatorium, Jim decides to combine the best of both farming and show business by turning a large New England farmhouse into a night club that will be open only on holidays. Jim reasons that he will be able to function as both a farmer and an entertainer and still have "three hundred and forty-seven days in which to kick around in."

After extensive planning and preparation, Jim's plush night spot (appropriately named the Holiday Inn) has its gala opening on New Year's Eve. Within a few hours, the inn becomes crowded with a huge group of fun seekers, and it becomes increasingly apparent to Jim that his idea will be an enormous success.

As the evening wears on, however, Jim's old buddy Ted staggers into the party in a very unhappy mood, looking desperately for a girl to dance with. The reason for Ted's depression is that he has just learned that his fiancée, Lila Dixon (Virginia Dale), has given him the air to marry a wealthy Texas oil baron.

Ambling around the dance floor, Ted happens upon a lovely young woman, Linda Mason (Marjorie Reynolds), and begins dancing with her, much to the delight of all the patrons. Jim, however, is less than delighted, because he has fallen in love with Linda.

Weeks later, Ted informs Jim that two Hollywood film producers want to make a movie about the Holiday Inn, featuring Ted and Linda in the leading roles. Jim opposes the idea, but he is forced to give in when Linda accuses him of trying to spoil a great opportunity for her.

During the next few months, Jim is disappointed to learn that Ted and Linda are not only the hottest thing in movies, but that they are also engaged to be married. Despairing, Jim turns to his maid, Mamie (Louise Beavers), for advice. She tells him that the best thing would be to tell Linda how much he loves her.

Deciding to follow Mamie's advice, Jim goes to Hollywood and discovers that Linda is miserably unhappy about her shallow Hollywood success and yearns for the days when she and Jim used to sit contentedly in front of the fireplace at Holiday Inn. When she learns that Jim has come to Hollywood to ask her to return with him, she cancels her movie contract and accompanies Jim back to the place where she was happiest. At first, this seems to leave poor Ted out in the cold, but at the last minute his former fiancée, Lila, returns from her romantic fiasco in Texas and informs Ted that this time she's back to stay.

Few musical films have ever been able to achieve *Holiday Inn*'s popularity. The reasons are clearly evident from the beginning to the closing scene. Bing Crosby and Fred Astaire spark memorable chemistry as a screen team, and each is superb in his specialties. The film's many impressive musical numbers (most notable of which are Crosby's sensitive handling of his biggest hit, "White Christmas," and Fred Astaire's beautiful dance duet with Marjorie Reynolds, performed to an instrumental version of Irving Berlin's "Be Careful, It's My Heart") are given an added gloss by the sharp delineation of David Abel's excellent monochrome photography.

The setting for the inn is a masterpiece of its kind. Designed by one of the cinema's most creative art directors, Hans Dreier, this set is a stunning example of rich colonial architecture, beautifully accented by a series of arched picture windows through which the Holiday Inn's spacious interiors can be easily viewed from outside. It is one of the most effective well-remembered scenic designs of the forties.

With Marjorie Reynolds

With Dorothy Lamour and Bob Hope

Road to Morocco
1942

CAST

Jeff Peters (BING CROSBY); Orville (Turkey) Jackson (BOB HOPE); Princess Shalmar (DOROTHY LAMOUR); Mullay Kasim (*Anthony Quinn*); Mihirmah (*Dona Drake*); Hyder Khan (*Vladimir Sokoloff*); Ahmed Fey (*Mikhail Rasumny*); Neb Jolla (*George Givot*); Oso Bucco (*Andrew Tombes*); Yusef (*Leon Belasco*); Kasim's Aide (*Jamiel Hasson*); Kasim's Aide (*Monte Blue*); Arabian Buyer (*Dan Seymour*); Arabian Waiter (*Ralph Penney*); First Guard (*George Lloyd*); Second Guard (*Sammy Stein*); Philippine Announcer (*Pete Katchenaro*); English Announcer (*Brandon Hurst*); Chinese Announcer (*Richard Loo*); Russian Announcer (*Leo Mostovoy*).

CREDITS

A Paramount Picture. Directed by David Butler. Associate Producer: Paul Jones. Original Screenplay by Frank Butler and Don Hartman. Director of Photography: William Mellor, A.S.C. Art Direction: Hans Dreier and Robert Usher. Film Editor: Irene Morra. Musical Director: Victor Young. Costumes by Edith Head. Process Photography by Farciot Edouart. Special Photography by Gordon Jennings. Sound Recording by Loren Ryder. New Songs by James Van Heusen and Johnny Burke.

SONGS

"Road to Morocco"
"Ain't Got a Dime to My Name (Ho-Hum)"
"Constantly"
"Moonlight Becomes You"

Running Time: 83 minutes

With Dorothy Lamour and Vladimir Sokoloff

With Edgar Blue Washington, Dorothy Lamour and Bob Hope

With Nick Shaid and Bob Hope

With Michael Mark and Bob Hope

With Bob Hope

After the enormous success of *Road to Zanzibar*, Paramount was now certain what kind of comic formula worked best for Bing Crosby and Bob Hope. This formula consisted of simply presenting the star duo as a couple of fast-talking swindlers who get themselves into terrible jams and are forced to flee to some dark, exotic locale where they become involved in almost every conceivable kind of wacky plot.

Paramount felt that this formula, which had served as a successful basis for a satire of jungle and adventure pictures, could be just as effective in a spoof of all the wartime Hollywood costume epics about Ali Baba, his forty thieves, and Princess Scheherazade. With this in mind, Paramount produced the third in the increasingly popular *Road* series, and *Road to Morocco* became perhaps the most famous of the series. It remains an exceptional piece of entertainment.

Road to Morocco is crammed with lavish pictorial delights, such as an impressive parade of dazzling costume designs by Edith Head and a plush Arabian palace conceived by Paramount's ace art director Hans Dreier. To enhance the stunning visuals, veteran songwriters James Van Heusen and Johnny Burke composed five of their loveliest, most lively tunes, including "Moonlight Becomes You," which Crosby croons to Dorothy Lamour in the palace garden.

Road to Morocco wastes no time in getting down to business. Crosby and Hope are introduced as survivors of a sunken steamship who are washed up on a beach along the Mediterranean. Befriending a wandering camel, the boys decide to head for Morocco in the hope of finding some adventure and romance. Stopping in one of the sleazier Moroccan provinces, they learn that food is scarce, money is tight, and the native Moroccans resent the intrusion of foreigners.

Just when Bing and Bob are about to give up

hope, a rotund pasha (Dan Seymour) offers Crosby six hundred "kolaks" if Bing will allow the pasha to take Bob to the palace of Princess Shalmar (Dorothy Lamour). Bing agrees, and the reluctant Hope is carted off to the palace by two strong-arm men.

A few hours later, the "ghost" of Bob's Aunt Lucy (actually Bob in hilarious drag) visits Crosby and chastises him for selling her nephew. Bing's conscience gets the best of him, and he decides to go looking for Bob in the palace of Shalmar.

Once there, Bing is flabbergasted to find his chum in the arms of the lovely princess. To top that off, Crosby learns that Bob has been chosen to become Shalmar's first husband ("I'm going to be her pasha," boasts Hope, "with an accent on the *pash!*"). Crosby decides to stick around the palace for a few more days.

Bing begins to woo the princess and is delighted when she begins to fall in love with him. She explains to Crosby, however, that it is written in the stars that Bob must be her husband, and nothing she may feel for Bing can stand in the way of destiny.

Everything changes, however, when the royal astrologer, Hyder Khan (Vladimir Sokoloff), tells the princess that a family of fireflies invaded his telescope lens and caused him to misread the stars. He tells her that it is no longer necessary for her to marry Hope.

Although this news delights Bing and the princess, complications develop when a cruel Arabian desert chieftain, Mullay Kasim (Anthony Quinn), learns of Shalmar's freedom and decides that he wants her for his own. Deciding to eliminate Hope and Crosby, Kasim binds their hands and feet and sends them out into the desert without food or water.

Several hours later, the boys are able to break their bonds. They make their way to Kasim's camp just before the marriage between Mullay and the reluctant Shalmar is about to take place. Inciting a riot between Kasim's men and a rival desert tribe, Crosby and Hope stop the ceremony and take the princess back to safety.

Weeks later, Crosby and Shalmar, along with Bob and his Moroccan girlfriend (Dona Drake), are on a luxury liner bound for the United States. Bob mistakes the ship's arsenal for a restroom and enters the volatile chamber with a lit cigarette dangling from his lips. The ensuing explosion leaves the cozy foursome drifting helplessly in the Atlantic on a crude raft.

After several days, Bob cannot stand it any longer, and he begins to come apart at the seams. "No food! No water! I can't stand it, I tell you!" screams Bob, acting out a nervous breakdown in a very dramatic and convincing manner. Crosby brings the hysterical Hope back to his senses when he tells him that they are approaching New York Harbor and there's nothing left to worry about.

Bob is anything but happy about the news. He turns to Bing and says, "Why'd you have to go and spoil the only good scene I got in the whole picture? If you'd only kept your mouth shut, I might've wound up with an Academy Award."

Road to Morocco received two Academy Award nominations, one for the brisk screenplay of Frank Butler and Don Hartman and the other for Loren Ryder's skillful sound recording.

Star-Spangled Rhythm
1942

CAST

Himself (BING CROSBY); Himself (BOB HOPE); Himself (RAY MILLAND); Himself (FRED MacMURRAY); Himself (ALAN LADD); Himself (DICK POWELL); Herself (DOROTHY LAMOUR); Herself (PAULETTE GODDARD); Herself (VERONICA LAKE); Herself (MARY MARTIN); Herself (VERA ZORINA); Herself (SUSAN HAYWARD); Himself (FRANCHOT TONE); Himself (ROCHESTER); Polly (BETTY HUTTON); William (Bronco Billy) Webster (VICTOR MOORE); Johnny Webster (EDDIE BRACKEN); Himself (LYNNE OVERMAN); Himself (WILLIAM BENDIX); Himself (JERRY COLONNA); Himself (CECIL B. DEMILLE); Himself (PRESTON STURGES); Himself (ALBERT DEKKER); Mr. DeSoto (WALTER ABEL).

CREDITS

A Paramount Picture. Directed by George Marshall. Associate Producer: Joseph Sistrom. Original Screenplay by Harry Tugend. Directors of Photography: Leo Tover, A.S.C., and Theodore Sparkuhl. Art Direction: Hans Dreier and Ernst Fegte. Set Decoration: Steve Seymour. Sound Recording by Harry Mills and John Cope. Film Editor: Paul Weatherwax. Musical Score and Direction by Robert Emmett Dolan. Costumes by Edith Head. Vocal Arrangements by Joseph J. Lilley. Dance Direction by Danny Dare. Sketches by George Kaufman, Arthur Ross, Norman Panama, and Melvin Frank. Songs by Harold Arlen and Johnny Mercer.

SONGS

"Time to Hit the Road to Dreamland"
"That Old Black Magic"
"Old Glory"
"A Sweater, a Sarong and a Peek-a-Boo Bang"
"Workin' on the Swing Shift"
"I'm Doing It for Defense"
"Sharp as a Tack"

Running Time: 99 minutes

During World War II, most major film studios contributed to the war effort by producing spirited, patriotic musical revues featuring all-star casts, a dozen or so popular songs, and enthusiastic flag waving. One of the best of these was Paramount's *Star Spangled Rhythm,* a rousing, slickly produced tribute to the armed forces, featuring every major Paramount star in a wide variety of comical sketches, blackouts, and musical numbers.

The film also featured an embryonic plot revolving around the genial studio gatekeeper (Victor Moore) and his efforts to secure the entire Paramount talent roster for a benefit performance. The old gent poses as the head of the studio and issues orders to all the stars, instructing them to quit work early and to congregate at a local auditorium.

The scheme is stifled when he is caught by a genuine studio executive (Walter Abel) and subsequently banned from the lot. The real executive tells the stars to disregard the unauthorized orders. However, when the stars learn that the benefit performance was to be for the crew of a navy destroyer, they decide to ignore the executive's order and go on with the performance. The resulting show is such an enormous success that the old gatekeeper is rehired as a studio employee and promoted. He becomes the hero of the entire Paramount lot.

The memorable finale of *Star Spangled Rhythm* was a musical tribute to the American flag entitled "Old Glory." It was appropriately set against an impressive studio mockup of Mount Rushmore and featured the voices of Bing Crosby plus a studio chorus, zestfully singing a tribute to America's colorful past. The number also featured a stirring, patriotic oration by Crosby, recounting the valiant deeds of Washington, Jefferson, and Lincoln.

Although the film is dated by today's standards, *Star Spangled Rhythm* remains a top-notch wartime entertainment. It provides the viewer with a fascinating insight into the public's taste in motion pictures during the Second World War. It is also an excellent opportunity to see several million dollars' worth of talent in one sitting.

"Old Glory"

Dixie

1943

CAST

Dan Emmett (BING CROSBY); Millie Cook (DOROTHY LAMOUR); Jean Mason (MARJORIE REYNOLDS); Mr. Bones (*Billy De Wolfe*); Mr. Whitlock (*Lynne Overman*); Mr. Felham (*Eddie Foy, Jr.*); Mr. Cook (*Raymond Walburn*); Jean's Father (*Grant Mitchell*); Jean's Mother (*Clara Blandick*); Mr. Devereaux (*Olin Howlin*); Homer (*Tom Herbert*); Mr. Masters (*Stanley Andrews*); Mr. La Plant (*Robert Warrick*); Mrs. Masters (*Hope Landin*); Mrs. La Plant (*Norma Varden*); Captain (*James Burke*); Lucius (*George H. Reed*); Drum Player (*Harry Barris*); Colonel (*Sam Flint*).

CREDITS

A Paramount Picture. Directed by A. Edward Sutherland. Associate Producer: Paul Jones. Screenplay by Darrell Ware and Karl Tunberg. Adaptation by Claude Binyon. Taken from a Story by William Rankin. Director of Photography: William Mellor, A.S.C. Art Supervision: Hans Dreier. Art Direction: William Flannery. Sound Recording: Earl Hayman and John Cope. Musical Direction: Robert Emmett Dolan. Filmed in Technicolor. Minstrel Costumes: Raoul Pene Du Bois. Film Editor: William Shea. Vocal Arrangements by Joseph J. Lilley. New Songs by James Van Heusen and Johnny Burke.

SONGS

"Sunday, Monday and Always"
"If You Please"
"A Horse That Knows the Way Back Home"
"She's From Missouri"
"Kinda Peculiar Brown"

Running Time: 89 minutes

With Tom Kennedy (in bartender's outfit) in a production shot

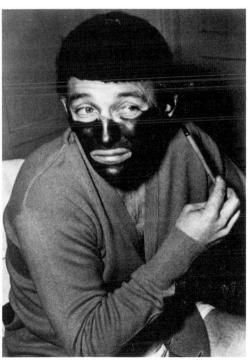

With Dorothy Lamour, Billy DeWolfe, Lynne Overman, Eddie Foy Jr.

Dixie was Bing Crosby's first film in Technicolor and is probably the definitive screen depiction of the minstrel show period. It is a superbly produced film that is as pleasing to the eye as it is to the ear.

Loosely based upon the life of the American songwriter and minstrel entertainer Daniel Decatur Emmett, *Dixie* is not so much a biography as it is an attempt to explain how the song "Dixie" (which Emmett composed in 1859) evolved into a ripsnorting Southern battle chant. Most of the incidents depicted in *Dixie* are romanticized embellishments having little to do with the real Dan Emmett. However, the film is successful in creating an aura of the old South that never fails to be convincing, thanks largely to the conviction expressed in the performances of Crosby, Marjorie Reynolds, Dorothy Lamour, and Billy De Wolfe and the elegant collection of stunning scenic designs by master art director Hans Dreier. The maestro's superb settings are endowed with an extra dimension by the rich Technicolor cinematography of veteran Hollywood cameraman William Mellor, and the songs of James Van Heusen and Johnny Burke complement the enterprise.

Unlike many other films, *Dixie* wisely avoids the temptation to present its characters as one-dimensional Southern stereotypes. Crosby and his co-stars do not even affect Southern accents; they play their roles in a straight and believable manner.

Dixie opens as unsuccessful songwriter Dan Emmett (Bing Crosby) leaves his Kentucky home to seek his fortune in New Orleans. After saying goodbye to his fiancée, Jean Mason (Marjorie Reynolds), Emmett boards a riverboat and encounters the flashy Mr. Bones (Billy De Wolfe). Engaging Emmett in a game of one-card draw, Mr. Bones cheats Dan out of all his money, then vanishes from sight as soon as the boat docks in New Orleans. Emmett pursues Bones to a posh New Orleans restaurant and threatens to beat his brains out, but Bones

With Billy DeWolfe

With Robert Warwick, Stanley Andrews and Olin Howlin

With Marjorie Reynolds

cools Emmett's flashing temper when he offers to treat the young songwriter to a meal.

Later, Emmett and Bones rent a room from a colorful old showman named Mr. Cook (Raymond Walburn). They soon find themselves vying for the affection of Cook's daughter Millie (Dorothy Lamour). Millie prefers Dan to Mr. Bones, and before long she and Emmett make wedding plans.

Returning home to explain his love for Millie to his fiancée, Dan is saddened to discover that Jean has fallen victim to the "paralyzing sickness" (probably polio). He marries her, out of a mixture of love and pity.

Moving to New York with his new bride, Dan sells a few of his songs to a publisher at a cut rate, but he refuses to sell his mellow tribute to the South entitled "Dixie."

Returning to New Orleans, Dan forms the first minstrel troupe, with the help of Mr. Bones, Mr. Cook, and two other talented showmen (Eddie Foy, Jr., and Lynne Overman). Meanwhile, Dan's former romance with Millie picks up again, and this makes Jean feel as though she's nothing but a painful burden to Emmett.

During one of the minstrel shows, Jean leaves Dan a note explaining that she has decided to step aside and allow Dan to marry Millie. Hearing of this, Millie sneaks into Emmett's dressing room and burns the letter, accidentally causing a fire to break out in the theater while Dan is delivering his slow-moving ballad "Dixie" on stage. Seeing the fire, Dan instructs the orchestra to pick up the tempo so that he can finish before the fire spreads. As a re-

sult, "Dixie" is transformed into a spirited Southern morale song, even though Emmett had written it as a low-keyed Southern ballad.

Not even pretending to be authentic history, *Dixie* does not present the incidents in Emmett's life as they actually happened and is probably better because of it. It is doubtful that the real Dan Emmett was so charming or romantic.

Among the film's many assets, the most outstanding elements in *Dixie* are Dreier's stylish settings, Mellor's impeccable photography, and the incredible array of fantastic costumes designed by Raoul Pene Du Bois. These costumes are uniformly excellent, from the gaudy minstrel outfits Crosby and his troupe wear during their stage performances, to a beautiful silvery top hat Billy De Wolfe sports during his early scenes with Crosby. The picture's mellow Southern flavor is further accented by the photography. William Mellor cleverly chose to dominate his superb Technicolor camerawork with colors truly suggestive of the warm, dreamy atmosphere of the old South. These include rich colonial whites, deep forest greens, and majestic sky blues and Confederate grays. The songs of Dan Emmett, including the title tune and the memorable "Old Dan Tucker," are as bright and fresh as ever, and the newer songs of James Van Heusen and Johnny Burke add to the overall effectiveness of *Dixie*. Most memorable among the Burke and Van Heusen tunes is the touching love ballad "Sunday, Monday, or Always," one of the nicest songs Bing has ever sung on screen.

Going My Way
1944

CAST

Father Chuck O'Malley (BING CROSBY); Genevieve Linden (*Rise Stevens*); Father Fitzgibbon (*Barry Fitzgerald*); Father Timothy O'Dowd (*Frank McHugh*); Ted Haines, Sr. (*Gene Lockhart*); Max Dolan (*William Frawley*); Ted Haines, Jr. (*James Brown*); Carol James (*Jean Heather*); Mr. Belknap (*Porter Hall*); Tomasso Bozzani (*Fortunio Bonanova*); Mrs. Carmody (*Eily Malyon*); Pee-Wee (*George Nokes*); Officer McCarthy (*Tom Dillon*); Tony Scaponi (*Stanley Clements*); Herman Langerhanke (*Carl Switzer*); Pitch Pipe (*Hugh Maguire*); Maid (*Sybil Lewis*); Mr. Van Heusen (*George McKay*); Mr. Lilley (*Jack Norton*); Mrs. Quimp (*Anita Bolster*); Fireman (*Jimmie Dundee*); Mother Fitzgibbon (*Adeline Reynolds*); Churchgoer (*Gibson Gowland*).

CREDITS

A Paramount Picture. Produced and Directed by Leo McCarey. Screenplay by Frank Butler and Frank Cavett. Original Story by Leo McCarey. Director of Photography: Lionel Lindon, A.S.C. Art Direction: Hans Dreier and William Flannery. Set Decoration: Gene Merritt and John Cope. Sound Recording by Steve Seymour. Film Editor: LeRoy Stone. Musical Director: Robert Emmett Dolan. Special Effects by Gordon Jennings. Costumes by Edith Head. Song: "Too-ra-loo-ra-loo-ra," by J. R. Shannon. New Songs by James Van Heusen and Johnny Burke.

SONGS

"Too-ra-loo-ra-loo-ra"
"Day After Forever"
"Going My Way"
"Swingin' on a Star"

Running Time: 130 minutes

With Barry Fitzgerald and Jean Heather

With Gene Lockhart

With Anita Bolster and James Brown

With Porter Hall

With Frank McHugh and Barry Fitzgerald

In 1944 Paramount released two of its most famous and popular films. One of them was the hard-hitting drama *Double Indemnity*. The other, *Going My Way,* was the complete opposite of *Double Indemnity* in story and mood but similar in featuring a well-known star in an unusual—for him—screen role.

A simple and unpretentious film about a spirited young priest and his unselfish efforts to make life more pleasant for others, *Going My Way* presented Bing Crosby with his first real change of pace since *Sing You Sinners*. Of course, Crosby's success in the role of the easy-going Roman Catholic priest named Father Chuck O'Malley has become well-known Hollywood history, and it would be redundant to analyze it here.

The excellence of Crosby and his co-star, Barry Fitzgerald, in the film's leading roles has, however, had a tendency to overshadow the fact that *Going My Way* is a personal tour-de-force for its writer-director, Leo McCarey. Realizing that the massive Frank Butler–Frank Cavett screenplay would amply fill more than two hours of screen time, McCarey wisely opted to direct the film at a brisk and flowing pace. The result is excellent cinema that sustains an audience's interest. McCarey had the considerable aid of cameraman Lionel Lindon, whose dark and artful black-and-white visuals are used to excellent effect (particularly in the closing shot of Crosby leaving the church, while the sweet strains of "Too-ra-loo-ra-loo-ra" play softly in the background).

Going My Way begins at a small New York church, Saint Dominic's. The parish has been suffering from overdue mortgages, bad management, and disenchanted parishioners during the previous few years. The main reason for this misfortune is that the church's curate of forty-five years, the aging, cantankerous Father Fitzgibbon (Barry Fitzgerald), has begun to lose his ability to sermonize.

With Rise Stevens and Fortunio Bonanova

With Tom Dillon

Realizing this, the archbishop dispatches a younger, more liberal priest, Father Chuck O'Malley (Bing Crosby), to Saint Dominic's in the hope that he will be able to get the ailing parish back on its feet. However, the older priest is violently opposed to any new religious ideas and begins to resent O'Malley's presence. Sensing the old man's disapproval, Father Chuck decides to straighten things out for the church without the old priest's knowledge.

Father O'Malley submits one of the songs he has composed to a music publisher, Max Dolan (William Frawley). Although Max feels that the song has charm, he explains to O'Malley that it is too "schmaltzy" to appeal to the general public. Disappointed but undaunted, O'Malley performs one of his jauntier compositions, a catchy number called "Swingin' on a Star." To his surprise, Max agrees to publish it. After thanking Max, Father Chuck instructs him to deliver the money for the song via the collection box at Saint Dominic's.

With the church back on its feet, Father Fitzgibbon begins warming up to Father O'Malley. He reveals to the young pastor that the greatest dream of his life is to visit his ninety-year-old mother in Ireland. O'Malley tells the old fellow that he'll be glad to look after things while Fitzgibbon is away in Ireland. However, O'Malley's friend Father O'Dowd (Frank McHugh) rushes in with the terrible news that Saint Dominic's is burning. Running outside to see for themselves, O'Malley and Fitzgibbon watch as half the city's fire department struggles to save the crumbling church from utter destruction. When Father O'Malley sees that this is impossible, he comforts the elderly priest, assuring him that they will be able to build again. But this does nothing to ease Fitzgibbon's grief. The old man becomes heartsick and subsequently bedridden.

All is set right, however, when O'Malley arranges for the church choir to go on a singing tour with Metropolitan Opera star Genevieve Linden (Rise Stevens). With the money earned from the tour, O'Malley is not only able to begin reconstruction on Saint Dominic's, but also brings Father Fitzgibbon's wizened mother to America for a tearful reunion with her son. Realizing that his work at Saint Dominic's has been accomplished, Father O'Malley quietly packs his grip and walks off into the night.

Bing Crosby revealed in his autobiography that Paramount had mixed feelings about allowing him to appear as a priest. The studio found it difficult to visualize thir number-one musical star in such an atypical role, and they were naturally concerned about how the filmgoing public would react. Of course, Paramount's fears proved groundless, and as everyone knows, *Going My Way* went on to become the studio's most successful film since Cecil B. De-Mille's *Reap the Wild Wind*. In addition, the film was later labeled one of the true classics of the 1940s and has also enjoyed tremendous success during its many revivals on television.

Its lasting popularity is, of course, due in part to the masterful direction of Leo McCarey, but it is really the magical screen chemistry between Bing Crosby and Barry Fitzgerald that makes *Going My Way* unforgettable. All their scenes together are superb, but the one that lingers in the memory is the one in which Crosby attempts to tell a disbelieving Fitzgerald that a number of Saint Dominic's younger parishioners have been accused of hijacking a poultry truck and stealing the turkeys. "Nonsense," retorts Fitzgerald, as he eagerly prepares to sit down to a delicious turkey dinner. "I'll have you know that the very food before us was donated to the parish by two of the boys that you say have been accused of stealing. I gave them both my blessing."

Crosby subtly replies, "And they gave you the bird."

With Betty Hutton

Here Come the Waves
1944

CAST

Johnny Cabot (BING CROSBY); Susan/Rosemary Allison (BETTY HUTTON); Windy (SONNY TUFTS); Ruth (*Ann Doran*); Tex (*Gwen Crawford*); Dorothy (*Noel Neill*); Lieutenant Townsend (*Catherine Craig*); Isabel (*Marjorie Henshaw*); Ensign Kirk (*Mae Clarke*); Bandleader (*Harry Barris*); Commodore (*Oscar O'Shea*); Dancer (*Roberta Jonay*); Dancer (*Guy Zanett*); First Fainting Girl (*Mona Freeman*); Second Fainting Girl (*Carlotta Jelm*); Chief Petty Officer (*Jimmy Dundee*); Johnny Cabot Fan (*Lillian Bronson*); Shore Patrolman (*James Flavin*); Yellow Cab Driver (*Kit Guard*); Girl (*Yvonne De Carlo*).

CREDITS

A Paramount Picture. Produced and Directed by Mark Sandrich. Original Screenplay by Allan Scott, Ken Englund, and Zion Myers. Director of Photography: Charles Lang, Jr. A.S.C. Art Direction: Hans Dreier and Roland Anderson. Set Decoration: Ray Moyer. Musical Direction: Robert Emmett Dolan. Sound Recording by Hugo Grenzbach. Nonmilitary Costumes by Edith Head. Film Editor: Ellsworth Hoagland. Process Photography: Farciot Edouart. Special Effects: Gordon Jennings and Paul Lerpae. New Songs by Johnny Mercer and Harold Arlen.

SONGS;

"My Mama Thinks I'm a Star"
"I Promise You"
"Let's Take the Long Way Home"
"Here Come the Waves"
"There's a Fellow Waiting in Poughkeepsie"
"Accentuate the Positive"

Running Time: 99 minutes

With Sonny Tufts

With Sonny Tufts, Betty Hutton and Noel Neill (in dark service suits)

With Noel Neill, Sonny Tufts and chorus

150

Here Come the Waves begins as singing idol Johnny Cabot (Crosby) and his chum Windy (Sonny Tufts) meet a singing-sister act known as the Allison Twins (Betty Hutton in a dual role). After talking to the twins for a few minutes, Johnny gets the impression that Susie Allison worships the ground he walks on but Rosemary thinks he is nothing more than a glorified ham.

Later, Johnny joins the navy, hoping to be assigned to destroyer duty with his pal Windy. Susan and Rosemary also join the navy, and fearing for Johnny's safety, Sue arranges for him to be assigned to direct all the benefit shows given by the Waves. Johnny resents this assignment, but his outlook begins to change when he and Rosemary begin falling in love during rehearsals for an upcoming Wave show.

Hearing about the romance between Johnny and Rosemary, Windy becomes jealous. He tells Rosemary that Johnny asked to be put in charge of the wave productions to escape the hazards of battle. After hearing this, Rosemary tells a puzzled Johnny that she never wants to see him again.

Meanwhile, Johnny learns that Susie was responsible for his unwelcome transfer. He decides to disobey regulations and board a destroyer against his prior orders. Hearing about Johnny's plan, Susie confesses everything to Rosemary and then quickly makes her way to Johnny's hotel room, hoping she can stop him from leaving. Once there, however, Susie discovers that Johnny has made up his mind to board the destroyer and that nothing she can say will change his mind.

Johnny dons a pair of dark glasses and a fake beard to disguise himself from his admirers. However, as soon as he sets foot on the street Susan reveals who the mysterious bearded gentleman is. Johnny's fans mob him, and he is rendered powerless to carry out his plan.

Returning to the navy base with Susan, Johnny is pleased to learn that Rosemary has learned the truth about his transfer and that she takes back everything she said about him. Windy and Susan also discover their hidden affection for each other, and the film ends in a forgivably contrived manner as Johnny and Windy appear on a giant motion-picture screen waving goodbye to Rosemary and Susan from the deck of a departing destroyer.

Although the film admittedly contains more than its share of enthusiastic flag waving, *Here Come the Waves* is still a clever spoof of what life is supposedly like for a popular crooning idol. Crosby appears as a tongue-in-cheek version of himself—a popular singer who is the idol of millions, the nation's biggest recording star, and a top box-office attraction, who even has special chocolate sundaes named after him.

This spoof gives Crosby a refreshing opportunity to satirize himself, Sinatra, Dick Powell, and other singing stars whose mellow tones were adored by millions. In one amusing sequence, Crosby makes a personal appearance at a theater and causes most of the bobby-soxers in the audience to faint by singing a balmy arrangement of "That Old Black Magic." In this hilarious tongue-in-cheek sequence, the Bingle was obviously spoofing his young competitor from Hoboken who had just such an effect upon the nation's bobby-soxers.

Here Come the Waves also has a great deal going for it in technical areas. These include superb direction (by *Holiday Inn* veteran Mark Sandrich) and marvelous art direction (particularly the crude, cartoonlike, realistically dingy backdrops for the many Wave shows in the film) that demonstrates that Hans Dreier's skills were not limited to designing quaintly beautiful farmhouses and gorgeous white riverboats.

Here Come the Waves makes one wish that Crosby and Betty Hutton had been given more chances to work together. Their contrasting screen personalities complement each other, and their romantic duet of the pulsating "I Promise You" is excellent. Sonny Tufts also shines as Crosby's sidekick (in a role that might have been written with Bob Hope in mind), and he takes full advantage of his opportunity to join Crosby in a spirited rendition of the Oscar-nominated song "Accentuate the Positive."

With Martha Sleeper

With Joan Carroll

With Ingrid Bergman

The Bells of St. Mary's

1945

CAST

Father Chuck O'Malley (BING CROSBY); Sister Benedict (INGRID BERGMAN); Mr. Bogardus (*Henry Travers*); Sister Michael (*Ruth Donnelly*); Patsy (*Joan Carroll*); Patsy's Mother (*Martha Sleeper*); Joe Gallagher (*William Gargan*); Dr. McKay (*Rhys Williams*); Eddie (*Dickie Tyler*); Mrs. Breen (*Una O'Connor*); Tommy (*Bobby Frasco*); Clerk (*Matt McHugh*); Delphine (*Edna Wonacott*); Luther (*Jimmy Crane*); Landlady (*Minerva Urecal*); Old Lady (*Cora Shannon*); The Sisters (*Gwen Crawford, Aina Constant, Eva Novak*).

CREDITS

A Rainbow-RKO Picture. Produced and Directed by Leo McCarey. Screenplay by Dudley Nichols. Original Story by Leo McCarey. Director of Photography: George Barnes, A.S.C. Art Direction: William Flannery. Set Decoration: Darrell Silver. Musical Score: Robert Emmett Dolan. Costumes by Edith Head. Film Editor: Harry Marker. Sound Recording by Stephen Dunn. Special Photography by Vernon L. Walker. Song: "The Bells of St. Mary's," by A. Emmett Adams and Douglas Furber. Other Songs by James Van Heusen, Johnny Burke, Grant Clarke, and George W. Meyer.

SONGS

"Aren't You Glad You're You?"
"The Bells of St. Mary's"
"In the Land of Beginning Again"

Running Time: 126 minutes

With Ruth Donnelly and Ingrid Bergman

The Bells of St. Mary's reintroduced *Going My Way's* protagonist Father Chuck O'Malley (Bing Crosby). The story begins as the spirited young priest is about to take over as pastor of the financially ailing Saint Mary's Cathedral and Parochial School. His principal task is to talk an aging businessman named Bogardus (Henry Travers) into donating a new school building to Saint Mary's.

O'Malley goes to visit Bogardus and bluntly asks the old man if he will give the new building to the church. Bogardus informs O'Malley that he has lived his entire life in the business world and that donating such an expensive building to any charity is out of the question. Furthermore, Bogardus says, his ailing heart might not be able to stand the strain of what such an enormous contribution could do to his finances.

O'Malley suggests to Bogardus that giving the building to such a worthwhile cause might do his heart more good than harm. O'Malley asks Bogardus to think it over for a week or so, and the old man agrees to let the young priest know when he comes to a decision.

A week later, Bogardus visits the Mother Superior at Saint Mary's, Sister Benedict (Ingrid Bergman), and informs her that he has decided to give the building to the church after all. He tells her that his decision has made a new man of him and that for the first time in thirty years, he is not bothered by heart trouble.

Just when everything seems to be looking up, however, Sister Benedict is suddenly taken ill and is confined to her quarters in the convent. After examining the ailing nun, the parish doctor (Rhys Williams) informs O'Malley that Sister Benedict has a mild strain of tuberculosis and must be transferred to a healthier climate. Not wanting the sister to be told anything that might crush her spirit, the doctor instructs O'Malley not to tell her about the TB but to have the archbishop quietly transfer her. O'Malley protests that transferring her without telling her why would probably break her heart. But the doctor insists that telling the sister about her malady would only complicate matters.

Upon learning that she is being forced to leave Saint Mary's, Sister Benedict becomes heartsick and confused. O'Malley sets the record straight by telling Sister Benedict the truth.

The Bells of St. Mary's was marked by numerous off-screen ironies during its production. For instance, its director and both of its stars won Oscars during its shooting, and two of those Oscars were for the film's predecessor, *Going My Way*. Furthermore, William Flannery's superbly deteriorated cathedral set was later incorporated effectively into a chilling Val Lewton–Boris Karloff horror film entitled *Bedlam*.

Like its esteemed predecessor, *The Bells of St. Mary's* bears the sentimental trademark of its producer-director, Leo McCarey. Proving once again that he was perhaps the only director in Hollywood who could make unbridled schmaltz palatable, McCarey injected the film with many tear-jerking and heart-tugging interludes and once again displayed his remarkable talent for telling a simple and uncomplicated story in a somehow profound and deeply moving manner. Of course, he was aided considerably by the superbly restrained performances of Bing Crosby and Ingrid Bergman as Father O'Malley and Sister Benedict. Both performers were excellent, and the final scene in which O'Malley compassionately tells Sister Benedict that she has tuberculosis perhaps best reveals why Crosby and Bergman were the leading box-office attractions of the period.

With Bob Hope

Road to Utopia

1946

CAST

Duke Johnson (BING CROSBY); Chester Hooton (BOB HOPE); Sal (DOROTHY LAMOUR); Ace Larson (*Douglas Dumbrille*); Kate (*Hillary Brooke*); Le Bec (*Jack La Rue*); Sperry (*Robert Barrat*); McGuirk (*Nestor Paiva*); Mr. Latimer (*Will Wright*); Narrator (*Robert Benchley*); Henchman (*Jimmy Dundee*); Newsboy (*Billy Benedict*); Purser (*Arthur Loft*); Boat Captain (*Alan Bridge*); Top Hat (*Romaine Callender*); Ship's Purser (*Paul Newlan*); Master of Ceremonies (*Edward Emerson*); Hotel Manager (*Ronnie Rondell*); Waiter (*George McKay*); Ringleader (*Larry Daniels*); Bear (*Charlie Gemora*).

CREDITS

A Paramount Picture. Produced by Paul Jones. Directed by Hal Walker. Screenplay by Norman Panama and Melvin Frank. Director of Photography: Lionel Lindon, A.S.C. Art Direction: Hans Dreier and Roland Anderson. Set Decoration: George Sawley. Musical Director: Robert Emmett Dolan. Musical Score by Leigh Harline. Sound Recording by Hugo Grenzbach. Dance Direction: Danny Dare. Costumes by Edith Head. Process Photography by Farciot Edouart. Film Editor: Stuart Gilmore. New Songs by James Van Heusen and Johnny Burke.

SONGS

"Goodtime Charlie"
"Welcome to My Dream"
"Would You?"
"It's Anybody's Spring"
"Personality"
"Put It There, Pal"

Running Time: 90 minutes

With Bob Hope

With Jim Thorpe (left), Bob Hope, and Harry Semels

With Bob Hope

Apparently deciding to make *Road to Utopia* the most outrageous entry in the series, screenwriters Norman Panama and Melvin Frank (who began their careers as jokesmiths for Bob Hope's radio program) pulled out all the comic stops, injecting the script with an almost incredible amount of the zaniest comedic devices imaginable. Crosby and Hope are seen as two shady vaudevillians on the run from a backfired swindle in San Francisco. Shipbound for Alaska, they steal the deed to an Alaskan gold mine from two ruthless killers named Sperry (Robert Barrat) and McGuirk (Nestor Paiva). Assuming the killers' identities. Crosby and Hope arrive in Skagway and are immediately hired as bodyguards by Klondike racketeer Ace Larson (Douglass Dumbrille). Through their association with the gang leader they meet Dorothy Lamour, a pretty soloist in the chorus line at the local dance hall. Dorothy takes a liking to the boys and invites them to a midnight rendezvous in her boudoir. Crosby and Hope are naturally flattered, little dreaming that her real intention is to entice the deed from them.

Dorothy goes to work on Bob first, telling him how exciting it is to be in the arms of a famous criminal. ("Those beady eyes! That weak chin! Oh, kiss me, Sperry!") However, when she tries the same routine with Bing, her plan backfires, and she falls in love with him. Sensing this, Bing confesses that he and his friend are not really the murderers, but just harmless song-and-dance men.

Agreeing to split the gold mine three ways, Bob, Bing, and Dorothy prepare to leave Alaska. But then they encounter the real Sperry and McGuirk at the local hotel. The killers recognize Bob and Bing and prepare to slit their throats, but once again the boys are saved by their ability to think fast. The boys grab Dorothy, hop a sled, and head for the Arctic wasteland. Hot on their trail are not only Sperry and McGuirk, but also the angry Ace Larson and his gang. A madcap chase ensues as the

With Dorothy Lamour

With Dorothy Lamour, Bob Hope, Claire Jamer and Maxine Fife

murderous mob pursues Bob, Bing, and Dorothy across the Klondike and almost capture them, but for a break in the ice that allows Hope and Lamour to escape safely, but leaves Crosby behind to make a last stand. Believing Bing to be dead, Dorothy agrees to become Bob's wife.

The main body of the story is told in flashback preceded by a humorous prelude showing Bob Hope and Dorothy Lamour as a wealthy pair of octogenarians relaxing quietly in the plush sitting room of their rambling country estate. They recall fond remembrances of the gold mine that brought them their fortune and sadly recall the dear old friend lost in the process. Their nostalgic patter is suddenly interrupted by a familiar sound gently sifting into the house from the street below. As the sound becomes more audible, Dorothy recognizes it as the mellow intonations of Crosby softly crooning his old hit from the film *Dixie*—"Sunday, Monday, or Always." Dorothy exclaims: "Listen! That voice! It can't be!" In keeping with the famous feud, Hope reacts typically: "Who'd be sellin' fish at this hour?" Much to Bob's chagrin, in walks Bing, alive, well, and full of recollections about the trio's adventures in Alaska.

Road to Utopia makes the previous films in the series look tame. True, each of the previous episodes were noted for brief interludes of outrageousness, but none of them filled its entire running time with unceasing lunacy. *Road to Utopia* is ninety minutes of sheer madness—unobstructed and uncontrolled—even spilling over into a love scene between Bob Hope and Dorothy Lamour, which contains a commentary by a talking bass.

Of course, a few of the jokes may be hard for some to swallow. (For example, when Hope and Crosby are shoveling coal in the boiler room of an Alaskan steamer, a rotund gentleman attired in white tie and tails asks them for a light. "Who are you?" asks Hope. "Nobody," replies the stranger. "Are you in this picture?" inquires Bing. The gentleman takes a leisurely drag on his cigarette and says, "No, I'm just taking a shortcut to stage ten.") Whether one delights in this sort of craziness or finds the effect jarring is really a matter of personal taste.

One characteristic shared by all six of the original *Road* films (the seventh, *Road to Hong Kong*, is generally dismissed as a weaker entry) was a rich variety of colorful performances by a supporting cast of some of Hollywood's most stalwart character players. *Road to Utopia* was no exception. Douglass Dumbrille, who had menaced every major comedy team in motion pictures except Laurel and Hardy, provided Hope and Crosby with their most formidable foe since Anthony Quinn in *Road to Morocco* and proved once again that he was the movies' ideal comic villain. The lovely, liquid-eyed Hillary Brooke, who always seemed more at home as a seductive spy in films like *Ministry of Fear*, slipped into the role of a laconic, gum-chewing dance-hall dame with surprising naturalness. And Jack LaRue, whose stone-faced malevolence has graced more B pictures than anyone can count, was on hand as Dumbrille's partner in crime.

At the beginning, *Road to Utopia* seems to set *Road*-film history by allowing Bob Hope to end up with Dorothy Lamour. But the final scene still assures Bing the last word. After recalling the trio's Alaskan odyssey, the elderly Crosby prepares to depart, but Bob and Dorothy insist that he meet their son before leaving. "Oh, Junior!" hails Dorothy. In walks the son, a dead image of Crosby. Hope looks directly at the audience, grins slyly, and says, "We adopted him."

Blue Skies

1946

CAST

Johnny Adams (BING CROSBY); Jed Potter (FRED ASTAIRE); Mary O'Hara (*Joan Caulfield*); Tony (*Billy De Wolfe*); Nita Nova (*Olga San Juan*); Mack (*Frank Faylen*); Mary Elizabeth (*Karolyn Grimes*); Martha (*Victoria Horne*); Drunk (*Jack Norton*); Charles (*Roy Gordon*); Flo (*Joan Woodbury*); Tough Guy (*John Kelly*); Hatcheck Girl (*Roberta Jonay*); Cigarette Girl (*Mary Jane Hodge*); Stage Manager (*John Gallaudet*); Minister (*Neal Dodd*); Bill (*Cliff Nazarro*); Charlie (*Michael Brandon*); Valet (*Clarence Brooks*).

CREDITS

A Paramount Picture. Directed by Stuart Heisler. Produced by Sol C. Siegel. Screenplay by Arthur Sheekman. Adaptation by Allan Scott. From an Original Idea by Irving Berlin. Director of Photography: Charles Lang, Jr., A.S.C., and William Snyder, A.S.C. Art Direction: Hans Dreier and Hal Pereira. Set Decoration: Sam Comer and Maurice Goodman. Film Editor: Leroy Stone. Sound Recording by Hugo Grenzbach and John Cope. Musical Direction: Robert Emmett Dolan. Costumes by Edith Head. Filmed in Technicolor. Dance Direction: Hermes Pan. Vocal Arrangements by Joseph J. Lilley. Songs by Irving Berlin.

SONGS

"You Keep Coming Back Like a Song"
"Puttin' on the Ritz"
"Blue Skies"
"A Couple of Song and Dance Men"
"I've Got My Captain Working for Me Now"
"Everybody Step"

Running Time: 104 minutes

With Joan Caulfield

With Fred Astaire and Joan Caulfield

Rehearsing a scene with director Stuart Heisler and Karolyn Grimes

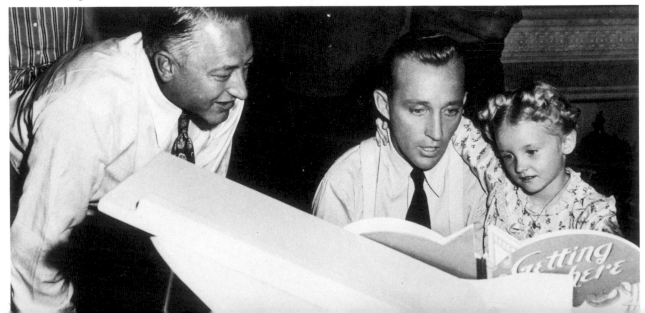

Blue Skies must be seen more than once to be fully appreciated. Apparently only a gushy love story cleverly draped around twenty Irving Berlin show tunes, the film at first gives the impression of being nothing more than an elaborate succession of musical routines performed by Bing Crosby and Fred Astaire. But on second viewing, *Blue Skies* reveals itself as an expertly produced and touching allegory about human relationships that uses a simple and entertaining premise to relate a message about life and love.

The film uses a standard love triangle involving Bing, Fred, and the lovely Joan Caulfield to illustrate that all romantic relationships involve compromise and that there are no "happy endings" in real life. To bring this message to life, director Stuart Heisler injects *Blue Skies* with a surprising amount of symbolism that makes the film much more interesting than it appears at first glance.

Blue Skies is also of interest to film students because it represents perhaps the apex of its studio's superb technical artistry during the 1940s. Thanks to the vibrant Technicolor camerawork of Charles Lang and William Snyder, the film outshines practically any Technicolor film Paramount had previously made, with the possible exception of Leisen's *Frenchman's Creek*. The film's technical excellence tends to overshadow its story of a young married couple who are forced to adjust their lives according to situations taking place around them.

Most of *Blue Skies* is presented in flashback. It begins as radio personality Jed Potter (Fred Astaire) relates the story of his life and career to his listeners. Jed had originally set out to be a dancer and had been considered one of the nation's leading hoofers for a number of years. Jed's story begins about the time that he and his friend Johnny Adams (Bing Crosby) were in competition with each other for the love of a beautiful chorus girl named Mary O'Hara (Joan Caulfield). Although

With Joan Caulfield

165

With Olga San Juan

With Billy DeWolfe

Jed had always hoped that Mary would choose him, it was really love at first sight for Mary and Johnny when they met at Johnny's small nightclub, the Flap-Jack.

Although Johnny warned Mary that he wasn't the marrying kind and that she would do better to forget him, Mary couldn't stay away from him, and they finally married. However, their life together was hardly a bed of roses and many times Mary walked out on Johnny. The main reason was that Johnny was an unstable businessman; he would buy and sell nightclubs at the drop of a hat. This irresponsible behavior really hadn't bothered Mary until the arrival of their daughter, Mary Elizabeth (Karolyn Grimes). Although Johnny also loved his child very much, he still couldn't bring himself to settle down with one nightclub, and as a result Mary and Johnny soon divorced.

Sometime later, Mary became engaged to Jed, who had gained a reputation as one of the best dancers in the business. As fate would have it, however, Johnny soon found himself unable to stay out of Mary's life after seeing what a beautiful young lady his daughter had become. Unable to resist Johnny's pleas, Mary broke off her engagement to Jed, and Jed took to the bottle.

During this period of Jed's life he began drinking on the job, and this led to a tragic accident, during a stage performance of the song "Heat Wave," that left him crippled and unable to continue his career.

At this point, the scene shifts back to Jed Potter at the radio station. He puts a philosophical capper on his story by saying, "That cured Jed Potter of drinking. . . . He never danced again." Jed goes on to say that Mary vanished from sight shortly after his accident and that neither he nor Johnny ever heard from her again.

Jed turns the program over to his friend Johnny, who sings Irving Berlin's "You Keep Coming Back Like a Song." At the last minute, Mary surprises Jed and Johnny by showing up out of nowhere, and the final scene finds Jed, Johnny, and Mary walking happily out of the studio.

In spite of its improbable ending, *Blue Skies* is a film of style and appeal. Its plot gets a bit corny now and then, but the sensitive portrayals of Astaire, Caulfield, and especially Crosby make many of the film's soapy moments seem believable. Crosby turns in an excellent performance as the irresponsible nightclub owner, and his scenes with Joan Caulfield and little Karolyn Grimes contain that special brand of touching sensitivity that only Crosby is capable of projecting on the screen. The poignancy of these scenes is heightened by musical director Robert Emmett Dolan's skillful use of a beautiful instrumental version of Irving Berlin's haunting love ballad "You Keep Coming Back Like a Song," which plays softly in the background during virtually all of Bing's poignant encounters with his wife and daughter.

Hans Dreier's scenic designs are, of course, masterful. The art director outdoes himself with the stunning setting for one of Crosby's smaller nightclubs, the Song Book. This nightclub set is one of Dreier's most striking creations. Its interiors are a superb combination of dark wooden paneling expertly decorated with rich purple tapestry, and its small stage area is given added beauty by the presence of a gigantic replica of a song book just behind the proscenium.

With Barry Fitzgerald

With Joan Caulfield

168

Welcome Stranger

1947

CAST

Dr. James Pearson (BING CROSBY); Trudy Mason (JOAN CAULFIELD); Dr. Joseph McRory (BARRY FITZGERALD); Emily Walters (*Wanda Hendrix*); Bill Walters (*Frank Faylen*); Mrs. Gilley (*Elizabeth Patterson*); Dr. Ronnie Jenks (*Larry Young*); Roy Chesley (*Robert Shayne*); Nat Dorkas (*Percy Kilbride*); Charles Chesley (*Charles Dingle*); Mort Elkins (*Don Beddoe*); Congressman Beeker (*Thurston Hall*); Mr. Daniels (*Paul Stanton*); Ben (*Milton Kibbee*); Clarence (*Clarence Muse*); Pinkett (*Charles Middleton*); Man on Train (*Erville Alderson*); Mr. Cartwright (*John Westley*); Mr. Weaver (*Edward Clark*); Mrs. Sims (*Ethel Wales*).

CREDITS

A Paramount Picture. Directed by Elliot Nugent. Produced by Sol C. Siegel. Screenplay by Arthur Sheekman. Original Story by Frank Butler. Director of Photography: Lionel Lindon, A.S.C. Art Direction: Hans Dreier and Franz Bachelin. Set Decoration: Sam Comer and John McNeil. Film Editor: Everett Douglas. Sound Recording by Stanley Cooley and Joel Moss. Costumes by Edith Head. Musical Director: Robert Emmett Dolan. New Songs by James Van Heusen and Johnny Burke.

SONGS

"Smile Right Back at the Sun"
"Country Style"
"As Long as I'm Dreaming"
"My Heart Is a Hobo"
"Smack in the Middle of Maine"

Running Time: 107 minutes

With Joan Caulfield

As *Welcome Stranger* begins, Dr. Joseph McRory (Barry Fitzgerald) is resentful of his new assistant, Dr. James Pearson (Bing Crosby). Not only does McRory object to Pearson's manner and dress, but the old man also can generate little respect for a doctor who sings.

Pearson is attracted to Trudy Mason (Joan Caulfield), a pretty young schoolteacher who does volunteer work in McRory's clinic. But Trudy rebuffs Pearson's advances, explaining that she is engaged to the local pharmacist. Sensing the animosity of Dr. McRory, Miss Mason, and the townspeople, Pearson decides to leave. But Mrs. Gilly (Elizabeth Patterson), McRory's maid and the only person in town who likes Pearson, pleads with the young doctor to talk things out with McRory. Deciding to follow her advice, Pearson joins McRory on one of the latter's fishing jaunts in the country. During this time, McRory becomes fond of Pearson and subsequently asks him to change his mind about leaving.

Several weeks later, McRory suffers a burst appendix and nearly dies, but Pearson's surgical skill saves him, and Pearson becomes a hero in the eyes of the townspeople.

Meanwhile, the head of the town council, Mr. Chesley (Charles Dingle), has imported a snobbish medical neophyte, Dr. Ronnie Jenks (Larry Young), to act as chief of surgery in the town's beautiful new hospital—a position originally promised to McRory. Several days later, Dr. Jenks receives the news of a disabling illness that has suddenly immobilized four students at a local school. About ten minutes after Jenks examines the children, Pearson and McRory arrive on the scene, to find that Jenks has diagnosed the children's malady as equine encephalitis, a virus brain fever contracted from infected horses. But McRory and Pearson have some ideas of their own. To confirm their suspicions, the two slip quietly into the school locker room and find four half-smoked cigars care-

With Joan Caulfield

lessly discarded in a nearby washbasin. McRory tells Chesley the real reason behind the boys' sickness, discrediting Jenks's diagnoses, and hence is given the position of chief of surgery for the new hospital.

Welcome Stranger, an underrated little picture, is as charming a film as Bing Crosby has ever appeared in. Crosby and his co-stars play their roles with complete conviction, and Barry Fitzgerald is superb as the elder physician who proves that feeling is often more important than knowledge. The film's main fault is its tendency to focus almost exclusively on its two male stars, oblivious of a fine supporting cast. The talents of Frank Faylen and Charles Dingle are sadly wasted in flimsy, one-dimensional roles.

Road to Rio

1947

CAST

Scat Sweeney (BING CROSBY); Hot Lips Barton (BOB HOPE); Lucia Maria De Andrade (DOROTHY LAMOUR); Catherine Vail (*Gale Sondergaard*); Trigger (*Frank Faylen*); Tony (*Joseph Vitale*); Mr. Cardoso (*Nestor Paiva*); Johnson (*Robert Barrat*); Rodrigues (*Frank Puglia*); Cavalry Captain (*Jerry Colonna*); The Andrews Sisters (*Themselves*); Three Latin Musicians (*The Wiere Brothers*); Farmer (*Charles Middleton*); Captain (*Stanley Andrews*); Samson (*Tor Johnson*); Steward (*Donald Kerr*); Barber (*Gino Corrado*); Valet (*George Chandler*); Buck (*Ray Teal*).

CREDITS

A Paramount Picture. Directed by Norman Z. McLeod. Produced by Daniel Dare. Screenplay by Edmund Beloin and Jack Rose. Director of Photography: Ernest Laszlo. Art Direction: Hans Dreier and Earl Hedrick. Film Editor: Ellsworth Hoagland. Costumes by Edith Head. Musical Director: Robert Emmett Dolan. Dance Direction by Bernard Pearce and Billy Daniel. Makeup Supervision by Wally Westmore. Process Photography by Farciot Edouart. New Songs by James Van Heusen and Johnny Burke.

SONGS

"But Beautiful"
"You Don't Have to Know the Language"
"Apalachicola, Florida"
"For What?"
"Experience"

Running Time: 100 minutes

Relaxing between scenes

(Left) With Laverne, Maxene and Patty Andrews

With Frank Puglia (left), the Wiere Brothers (in the background) and Bob Hope

Unlike most other entries in the *Road* series, *Road to Rio* contains practically nothing in the way of talking animals, Hollywood "in" jokes, or outlandish sight gags. Its comedy is subdued for a *Road* film, and it almost never allows Crosby and Hope to indulge in any of the wacky shenanigans in such abundant display throughout the last three films of the series. But even though it strays far from the zany plot formula that had been used to such great effect earlier, *Road to Rio* somehow emerges as the best and in many ways the most unusual film of the series.

After the uninhibited insanity of *Road to Utopia*, Paramount probably felt that to attempt a higher level of zaniness in *Road to Rio* would be foolhardy and decided to present the fifth adventure as a relatively traditional musical comedy. *Road to Rio* focuses most of its attention on Crosby, Hope, its interesting plot, and its impressive roster of Burke–Van Heusen songs, instead of forcing these elements to share the spotlight with admittedly funny but often annoying wackiness.

Paramount wisely compensated for *Road to Rio*'s dearth of craziness by investing it with an excellent screenplay (by Edmund Beloin and Jack Rose) that bristles with some of the most clever dialogue in any *Road* picture. The studio also enlisted the services of the popular Andrews Sisters to act as vocal foils for Bing and the hilarious Wiere Brothers to act as comic foils for Bob.

In addition to probably being the best *Road* film, *Road to Rio* also boasts the cleverest set of opening titles, presented as an animated cartoon. The names of the film's three principal players, Bing Crosby, Bob Hope, and Dorothy Lamour, literally dance onto the screen while a lively Latin American band renders the ever-popular Samba song "Brasilia" in the background.

Immediately following these colorful opening titles, *Road to Rio* swings into action as two crooked

With Dorothy Lamour

With Bob Hope and the Wiere Brothers

With Bob Hope, Gale Sondergaard, Joseph Vitale and Frank Faylen

musicians (Hope and Crosby) accidentally set fire to a carnival and subsequently find it necessary to stow away aboard a luxury liner bound for Rio de Janeiro. During the ocean voyage, the boys befriend a beautiful and mysterious young woman named Lucia De Andrade (Dorothy Lamour), who is almost constantly in the company of her even more mysterious aunt, Catherine Vail (Gale Sondergaard). Although both Hope and Crosby are extremely attracted to Lucia, they soon discover that she is given to sudden and inexplicable changes in mood. At times, she is very friendly toward the boys, but less than an hour later she will insist that she hates them. Deciding to investigate the reasons for this strange behavior, Hope and Crosby learn that Lucia is under the hypnotic spell of her aunt and that she is being forced to marry a man she doesn't love, in Brazil. Hope and Crosby agree to keep a protective eye on Lucia as soon as the ship docks in Rio.

Several days later, the boys arrive in the beautiful South American city and search for work in nightclubs. To better their chances of finding a job in a Latin American locale, the boys befriend three talented but goofy Brazilian musicians (the Wiere Brothers) and are immediately hired by a big-time nightclub owner, Mr. Cardoso (Nestor Paiva). Just as they are about to start work, however, Bob and Bing discover that Cardoso hired the five of them because he thought they were Americans and that he wouldn't take it kindly if he found out that the Brazilian trio could not utter a word of English. Deciding to deceive Cardoso, Crosby and Hope teach each of the musicians an English expression ("You're telling me"; "This is murder"; and "You in the groove, Jackson") in the hope that this will enable the fellows to pass themselves off as Americans. Needless to say, the ploy fails, and Hope and Crosby, along with their three friends, are tossed out on their ears.

With the Wiere Brothers, Bob Hope and Nestor Paiva

A few days later, the boys learn that Lucia's wedding is about to take place. They decide to attend the affair disguised as a Caribbean pirate and a Carmen Miranda–like "gootchy-gootchy" dancer. Arriving at the wedding, the boys entertain the guests by doing a hilarious Latin American song-and-dance routine that fools everyone except Mrs. Vail's strong-arm men Trigger (Frank Faylen) and Tony (Joseph Vitale).

Forced to abandon their disguises, Hope and Crosby manage to obtain certain papers that enable Lucia to escape her unpleasant fate and cause Catherine Vail and her accomplices to be brought to justice. Bob asks Bing just what these documents contained that made them so important at the last minute. After thinking it over for a couple of seconds, Bing decides not to reveal their contents, explaining that "the world must never know."

Following this, Bob and Bing ask Lucia to reveal which of them she has chosen to marry. Much to Bing's surprise, Lucia names Bob as the lucky man.

Weeks later, Bing goes to visit Bob and Lucia in their Niagara Falls honeymoon suite and tells Bob that he still can't understand Lucia's choice of mate. Once Bing is out the door, however, he peers through the keyhole and discovers that Bob has been hypnotizing Lucia in the same manner as her Aunt Catherine.

Road to Rio is a gem of a comedy that contains more than its share of hilarity, despite the noticeable absence of any outlandish humor. Regretfully, it must be acknowledged that the film was the last great *Road* picture.

With Joan Fontaine

The Emperor Waltz

1948

CAST

Virgil Smith (BING CROSBY); Johanna Franziska Von Stultzenberg (JOAN FONTAINE); Baron Holenia (*Roland Culver*); Emperor Franz Joseph (*Richard Haydn*); Princess (*Lucile Watson*); Dr. Zwieback (*Sig Rumann*); Archduchess Stephanie (*Julia Dean*); Chamberlain (*Harold Vermilyea*); Chambermaid (*Roberta Jonay*); Obersthofmeister (*John Goldsworthy*); Tyrolean Girl (*Doris Dowling*); Abbe (*James Vincent*); Gamekeeper (*Harry Allen*); Von Usedon (*Frank Elliot*); Officer (*Paul de Corday*); Master of Ceremonies (*Jack Gargan*); Diplomat (*Cyril Delevanti*); Marquess (*Frank Corsaro*).

CREDITS

A Paramount Picture. Directed by Billy Wilder. Produced by Charles Brackett. Screenplay by Charles Brackett and Billy Wilder. Director of Photography: George Barnes, A.S.C. Filmed in Technicolor. Technicolor Director: Natalie Kalmus. Associate: Robert Brower. Art Direction: Hans Dreier and Franz Bachelin. Musical Score by Victor Young. Film Editor: Doane Harrison. Costumes by Edith Head. Makeup Supervision by Wally Westmore.

SONGS

"I Kiss Your Hand, Madame" (Fritz Rotter and Ralph Erwin)

"The Kiss in Your Eyes" (Richard Heuberger and Johnny Burke)

"Friendly Mountains" (Johnny Burke, based on Swiss airs)

"Get Yourself a Phonograph" (James Van Heusen and Johnny Burke)

"The Emperor Waltz" (Johnny Burke, based on music by Johann Strauss)

Running Time: 106 minutes

With Joan Fontaine

With Roland Culver

"The Emperor Waltz" is an intriguing paradox in the film career of director Billy Wilder. It ranks as possibly the most atypical film the director ever made.

Throughout his career, Wilder has always been known as a filmmaker with a penchant for examining the imperfections of humanity in a frank and often disturbing manner. Not surprisingly, many of the director's most impressive works have been harsh, cynical dissections of the evils and maladies of mankind. These have included warfare (in *Five Graves to Cairo*), greed and deception (in *Double Indemnity*), alcoholism (in *The Lost Weekend*), vanity (in *Sunset Boulevard*), and human sacrifice (in *Ace in the Hole*).

It is virtually impossible to believe that the man who made these films could also film a light romantic fantasy; yet *The Emperor Waltz* is precisely that. Containing not a single iota of cynicism, it is a pleasant, almost flowery fairy tale of the star-crossed romance between a cocky American phonograph peddler and an aristocratic Austrian countess. Under Wilder's direction, it emerges as a compelling love story, revealing for the first time a softer, less caustic dimension of the director's considerable talent. The film also benefits from the lush Technicolor photography of George Barnes and from the often poignant acting of Bing Crosby and Joan Fontaine as the socially incompatible lovers.

The film exudes a distinctive "story book" enchantment that is saved from being juvenile by the complete conviction with which it is presented. *The Emperor Waltz* is a kind of adult fairy story, admittedly overflowing with romantic idealism but still managing to depict the "perfect love" in such a way as to make it almost believable.

The film is set in Austria during the reign of Emperor Franz Joseph (Richard Haydn), and most of its action takes place in and around the emperor's resplendent palace in the Tyrolean Alps. Into this colorful locale comes Virgil Smith (Bing Crosby), a smooth-talking supersalesman from an American phonograph company. His assignment is to introduce the record player into the lives of the country's royalty, a task that soon proves difficult, even for Smith.

He is granted an appointment to see the emperor and gains access to the royal palace, but when he tries to demonstrate the phonograph, the palace guards mistake it for a bomb and quickly evict Smith from the premises.

However, Virgil is every inch a salesman and not easily daunted. He sets out to woo the emperor's favorite niece, Countess Johanna Von Stultzenberg (Joan Fontaine), hoping that she might succumb to his velvety charm and perhaps introduce him to her illustrious uncle. But the fashionable Johanna wants nothing to do with the smooth-tongued Smith. She tells him that seeing him socially would be far beneath her station and that she regards his cocky attitude and mannerisms as objectionable. Virgil realizes that her upbringing prevents her from consorting with anyone who isn't of royal blood. Although he resents her attitude, he reasons that it would be wise for him to leave her alone.

Unbeknownst to Virgil, his little dog, Buttons, has developed romantic notions about Johanna's pet poodle, a pure-bred, pampered canine whose ideas on class seem to be equal to those of her mistress. Buttons has made numerous attempts to acquaint himself with the pompous poodle, but his attentions have been met with growls and snaps that lead to combat. On more than one occasion, Virgil and the countess are compelled to act as peacemakers to prevent their dogs from killing each other. After the second hostile skirmish, Johanna's poodle becomes strangely withdrawn and moody. The countess surmises that her dog's neurotic behavior must be a result of her unfriendly encounters with Buttons. Johanna decides to take her poo-

dle to see Virgil's dog, in the hope that the animals will become better acquainted and form a friendly truce. After much coaxing, the dogs finally come together on peaceful terms and discover that they actually like each other. Virgil and Johanna make a similar discovery. They, too, begin to realize their hidden affection for each other after Virgil decides to stop being a wise guy and the countess decides to drop her aristocratic snobbery. After many trials and tribulations, Virgil and Johanna waltz their way to a happy ending.

A Connecticut Yankee in King Arthur's Court

1949

CAST

Hank Martin (BING CROSBY); Lady Alesande (RHONDA FLEMING); Sir Sagrimore (WILLIAM BENDIX); King Arthur (*Sir Cedric* HARDWICKE); Sir Launcelot (*Henry* WILCOXON); Merlin (*Murvyn Vye*); Sir Logris (*Joseph Vitale*); Sir Galahad (*Richard Webb*); Head Executioner (*Alan Napier*); Morgan Le Fay (*Virginia Field*); Lady Penelope (*Julia Faye*).

CREDITS

A Paramount Picture. Produced by Robert Fellows. Directed by Tay Garnett. Screenplay by Edmund Beloin. Based on an Original Story by Mark Twain. Director of Photography: Ray Rennahan. Art Direction: Hans Dreier and Roland Anderson. Set Decoration: Sam Comer and Bertrand Granger. Makeup Supervision by Wally Westmore. Process Photography by Farciot Edouart. Filmed in Technicolor. Costumes by Edith Head. Music by Victor Young. New Songs by James Van Heusen and Johnny Burke.

SONGS

"Once and for Always"
"If You Stub Your Toe on the Moon"
"When Is Sometime"
"Busy Doing Nothing"
"Twixt Myself and Me"

Running Time: 107 minutes

With William Bendix

With Rhonda Fleming

With Sir Cedric Hardwicke, Rhonda Fleming and William Bendix

A Connecticut Yankee in King Arthur's Court is one of Bing Crosby's most expensive and elaborate screen musicals. It is also the finest and most enjoyable film adaptation of the Mark Twain novel ever made.

Mark Twain's fantasy novel about the adventures of a modern American chap who is thrown back into the colorful and adventurous days of King Arthur and the Knights of the Round Table had been transferred to the screen on two occasions prior to Bing Crosby's 1949 version. The first of these was a well-made silent picture produced in 1920 and featuring Harry C. Myers as the title character; the second was filmed in 1931 with Will Rogers as the feisty and impetuous Yankee. Both these films were enjoyable and expertly produced (the Rogers version did exceptionally well at the box office and was listed as one of the Ten Best Films of 1930 by *The New York Times*), but neither of them managed to match the quality of the Bing Crosby version.

Both the Myers and Rogers versions were successful in bringing to the screen the many comic subtleties of Mark Twain's novel, but they lacked the outstanding art direction, set decoration, and photography that made the Crosby version so enjoyable. The grainy, yet creative cinematography of the first two films was interesting, but it was no match for Ray Rennahan's superb fantasy-oriented spectrum of Technicolor images, such as the beautiful, softly focused montage of Crosby and Rhonda Fleming as the Yankee and his lady singing the picture's pleasant love theme, "Once and for Always."

The picture also includes a spectacular studio recreation of Camelot designed by Hans Dreier and featuring an enormous medieval castle complete with spacious ballroom, courtyard, and outdoor jousting arena. Because it is a Bing Crosby vehicle, the film also boasts a colorful collection of songs, which Bing sings with Rhonda Fleming, William Bendix, and Sir Cedric Hardwicke.

A Connecticut Yankee in King Arthur's Court finds the Groaner in the role of Hank Martin, a happy-go-lucky New England blacksmith who is knocked unconscious when he and his pony collide with a tree during a violent rainstorm. Hank awakens, to find himself face to face with an Old World knight, who introduces himself as Sir Sagrimore (William Bendix) and informs Hank that he is one of King Arthur's Knights of the Round Table.

The disbelieving Hank accompanies Sagrimore to Camelot and is surprised to learn that the knight was telling the truth. Sagrimore then introduces Hank to King Arthur (Sir Cedric Hardwicke), his niece Lady Alesande (Rhonda Fleming), and history's most famous magician, Merlin (Murvyn Vye). Although Hank is intrigued by all he sees, he discovers that the people of Camelot regard him as a strange monster. Soon they begin demanding that he be burned at the stake.

This does not really concern Hank, however; he realizes that these people know nothing of the technology of Hank's time and would run in fright if he lit a match. Using a pocketful of kitchen matches, Hank dazzles the citizens of Camelot as he makes short bursts of fire jump between his fingers. Even Merlin is impressed, and within a few hours Hank is labeled a great and mighty wizard.

Not wanting to incur the wrath of this powerful wizard, King Arthur asks Hank if there is anything he wants. Hank replies that he'd like to open a small blacksmith shop on the outskirts of the kingdom. The king grants Hank's request, and the young fellow is soon the proprieter of a medieval blacksmith shop, with Sir Sagrimore (whom Hank now affectionately refers to as "Saggy") as his trusted assistant.

Meanwhile, Hank becomes infatuated with Lady Alesande and is pleased to learn that she returns his affection. She explains to Hank, however, that she is betrothed to the gallant Sir Launcelot (Henry Wilcoxon). But Hank has become thoroughly enamoured of Sandy, as he calls her, and insists upon going to see her at least once a day. To Hank's dismay, Sir Launcelot finds out about this and challenges the peaceloving blacksmith to a jousting match. Hank asks King Arthur if he may engage in the match using only his homemade lariat as a weapon. The king grants Hank's request, and during the jousting match, Sir Launcelot becomes entangled in Hank's lasso and rendered helpless.

Weeks later, Merlin and his accomplice Sir Logris (Joseph Vitale) try to take over the kingdom by kidnapping Lady Alesande and holding her prisoner at a castle in the country. Learning of this, Hank goes to rescue Sandy but receives a blow on the head in the process that transports him back to the present day.

A few months later, Hank goes to see a descendant of King Arthur and tells the old gentleman about his recent adventures in Camelot. Not quite knowing what to make of Hank's story but finding him a personable young man, the old lord tells Hank to visit the garden before he leaves so that he can meet King Arthur's great, great grandniece. Strolling into the garden, Hank is both surprised and delighted to discover that the girl is the image of his beloved Sandy.

Certainly one of the most appealing screen fantasies, *A Connecticut Yankee in King Arthur's Court* presents Bing with one of his longest and most rewarding comedy roles. He portrays Hank Martin as a compassionate as well as a jovial man.

Top O' the Morning

1949

CAST

Joe Mulqueen (BING CROSBY); Conn McNaughton (ANN BLYTH); Briany McNaughton (BARRY FITZGERALD); Hughie Devine (*Hume Cronyn*); Biddy O'Devlin (*Eileen Crowe*); Gillespie (*Tudor Owen*); Pearse O'Neill (*Jimmy Hunt*); Inspector Fallon (*John McIntire*); Larkin (*John Eldredge*); Gossip (*John Costello*); Clark O'Ryan (*Dick Ryan*); Maid (*Mary Field*).

CREDITS

A Paramount Picture. Directed by David Miller. Produced by Robert L. Welch. Screenplay by Edmund Beloin and Richard Breen. Director of Photography: Lionel Lindon, A.S.C. Art Direction: Hans Dreier and Henry Bumstead. Set Decoration: Sam Comer and Emile Kuri. Film Editor: Arthur Schmidt. Sound Recording by Philip Wisdom and Gene Garvin. Costumes by Mary Kay Dodson. Musical Direction: Robert Emmett Dolan. Vocal Arrangements by Joseph J. Lilley. Dance Direction: Eddie Prinz. Technical Adviser: Arthur Shields. Makeup Supervision by Wally Westmore. New Songs by James Van Heusen and Johnny Burke.

SONGS

"Top O' the Morning"
"Oh, 'Tis Sweet to Think"
"The Donovans"
"You're in Love With Someone"

Running Time: 100 minutes

With Barry Fitzgerald

Top o' the Morning was the third and final film featuring the team of Bing Crosby and Barry Fitzgerald. It emerged as a dull vehicle in which both Crosby and Fitzgerald were powerless to do much of anything.

Released in August 1949, *Top o' the Morning* finds Crosby in the role of an easygoing insurance sleuth who is called to Ireland when the precious Blarney Stone is looted. Fitzgerald, who appears as a cranky old Irishman, tries his best to remind the audience of good old Father Fitzgibbon from *Going My Way*. Unfortunately, both Crosby and Fitzgerald are defeated by the trivial material, and Fitzgerald in particular is unfortunate in his stereotyped role of a cantankerous old Irishman with a heart of gold. As a result, his performance is too broadly comic. This is not any fault of Fitzgerald's; his role is written in such a way that any actor would find it next to impossible to make the part believable.

With Ann Blyth

With Clarence Muse

Riding High

1950

CAST

Dan Brooks (BING CROSBY); Alice Higgins (*Colleen GRAY*); J. L. Higgins (*Charles* BICKFORD); Happy (*William* DEMAREST); Margaret (*Frances Gifford*); Racing Secretary (*James Gleason*); Professor Pettigrew (*Raymond Walburn*); Lee (*Ward Bond*); Whitey (*Clarence Muse*); Pop Jones (*Percy Kilbride*); Edna (*Margaret Hamilton*); Johnson (*Harry Davenport*); Eddie Howard (*Douglass Dumbrille*); J. P. Chase (*Gene Lockhart*); Mary Winslow (*Marjorie Lord*); Hamburger Man (*Irving Bacon*); Himself (*Joe Frisco*); Williams (*Frankie Darro*); Erickson (*Charles Lane*).

CREDITS

A Paramount Picture. Produced and Directed by Frank Capra. Screenplay by Robert Riskin. Based on a Story by Mark Hellinger. Additional Dialogue by Melville Shavelson and Jack Rose. Directors of Photography: George Barnes, A.S.C., and Ernest Laszlo, A.S.C. Art Direction: Hans Dreier and Walter Tyler. Set Decoration: Emile Kuri. Film Editor: William Hornbeck. Sound Recording by Hugo Grenzbach and John Cope. Costumes by Edith Head. Musical Direction by Victor Young. Musical Associate: Troy Sanders. Vocal Arrangements by Joseph J. Lilley. Process Photography: Farciot Edouart. Assistant Director: Arthur Black. New Songs by James Van Heusen and Johnny Burke.

SONGS

"Sunshine Cake"
"The Horse Told Me"
"Sure Thing"
"Some Place on Anywhere Road"

Running Time: 112 minutes

With Frances Gifford

With Clarence Muse and Frankie Darro

With Raymond Walburn, Coleen Gray, Clarence Muse and William Demarest

Superior to Crosby's previous screen outing, *Top o' the Morning*, *Riding High* is director Frank Capra's spirited and faithful remake of his own 1934 film hit *Broadway Bill*. It casts Bing in the colorful role of an easygoing horseplayer who constantly looks to his beloved horse for a victory on the turf. After many trials and tribulations the horse finally gives Crosby his long-awaited victory but dies in the process.

Riding High is not one of Frank Capra's outstanding contributions to the screen, but it is a believable and enjoyable glimpse at the world of professional horse racing. Everyone connected with the picture must either have been familiar with racing life or researched the topic thoroughly. As the film's easygoing protagonist, Bing is excellent in a nicely written role that shows what he is capable of when his material matches his talent.

Mr. Music

1950

CAST

Paul Merrick (BING CROSBY); Katherine Holbrook (*Nancy Olson*); Alex Conway (*Charles Coburn*); Jefferson Blake (*Robert Stack*); Haggerty (*Tom Ewell*); Lorna Marvis (*Ruth Hussey*); Aunt Amy (*Ida Moore*); Danforth (*Charles Kemper*); Carpenter (*Donald Woods*); Jerome Thisby (*Claude Curdle*); Himself (*Gower Champion*); Herself (*Marge Champion*); Himself (*Groucho Marx*); Herself (*Peggy Lee*); Herself (*Dorothy Kirsten*); Themselves (*The Merry Macs*).

CREDITS

A Paramount Picture. Directed by Richard Haydn. Produced by Robert L. Welch. Screenplay by Arthur Sheekman. Suggested by the Play by Samson Raphaelson. Director of Photography: George Barnes, A.S.C. Film Editor: Doane Harrison and Everett Douglas. Assistant Director: Harry Caplan. Special Effects by Farciot Edouart. Vocal Arrangements by Joseph J. Lilley. Musical Direction by Van Cleave. Dance Direction by Gower Champion. Songs by James Van Heusen and Johnny Burke.

SONGS

"Life Is So Peculiar"
"High on the List"
"Wouldn't It Be Funny"
"Wasn't I There?"
"Mr. Music"
"Once More the Blue and White"
"Milady"
"Then You'll Be Home"

Running Time: 110 minutes

With Peggy Lee

With Charles Coburn and Nancy Olson

With Groucho Marx

As every cinema student is aware, the 1950s saw a drastic drop in the public's interest in motion pictures. As a result, many film stars of the thirties and forties found that most of their screen vehicles produced during the fifties were financially unsuccessful. Bing Crosby was no exception, and most of his films produced after *A Connecticut Yankee in King Arthur's Court* are lacking the marvelous energy and spirit that had made his earlier motion pictures popular. Among the least satisfying is *Mr. Music*, an elaborate but weak picture that is a disappointing throwback to the days when the Bingle had to attempt to make the most of silly scripts and threadbare plots.

If anything can be said in favor of *Mr. Music*, it is that Crosby is able to turn in a top-notch performance that manages to hold the audience's attention despite the character's shallowness. Apart from Crosby's portrayal, however, the film has little to offer. The slow-moving film is also much longer than it should have been.

The story of *Mr. Music* is of little importance and consists of simply introducing Crosby as a golf-crazy songwriter who does not relish the long, solitary hours of concentration needed to compose winning lyrics. An aging producer (Charles Coburn) and an ambitious young secretary (Nancy Olson) do their best to get him back to the drawing board.

Here Comes the Groom

1951

CAST

Pete Garvey (BING CROSBY); Emmadel Jones (JANE WYMAN); Winifred Stanley (ALEXIS SMITH); Wilbur Stanley (Franchot TONE); Pa Jones (*James Barton*); George Degnan (Robert Keith); Suzi (*Beverly Washburn*); Bobby (*Jacky Gencel*); Ma Jones (*Connie Gilchrist*); McGonigle (*Walter Catlett*); Mr. Godfrey (*Alan Reed*); Mrs. Godfrey (*Minna Gombell*); Governor (*Howard Freeman*); Aunt Abby (*Maidel Turner*); Uncle Elihu (*H. B. Warner*); Uncle Prentiss (*Nicholas Joy*); Uncle Adam (*Ian Wolfe*); Mrs. McGonigle (*Ellen Corby*); Policeman (*James Burke*); Baines (*Irving Bacon*).

CREDITS

A Paramount Picture. Produced and Directed by Frank Capra. Screenplay by Virginia Van Upp, Liam O'Brien, and Myles Connolly. Original Story by Robert Riskin and Liam O'Brien. Art Direction: Hal Pereira and Earl Hedrick. Director of Photography: George Barnes, A.S.C. Film Editor: Ellsworth Hoagland. Costumes by Edith Head. Process Photography by Farciot Edouart. Musical Direction: Joseph J. Lilley. Song: "In The Cool, Cool, Cool of the Evening," by Johnny Mercer and Hoagy Carmichael. Other Songs by Jay Livingston and Ray Evans.

SONGS

"In The Cool, Cool, Cool of the Evening"
"Bonne Nuit"
"Your Own Little House"
"Misto Christofo Columbo"

Running Time: 113 minutes

With Alexis Smith

With Jack Gencel and Beverly Washburn

With Frank Fontaine, Cass Daley, Dorothy Lamour and Louis Armstrong

With Jane Wyman

Here Comes the Groom features Crosby as a big-hearted journalist who becomes involved in a romantic triangle when he and Franchot Tone actively pursue the lovely Jane Wyman. Following the usual chain of events for films of this type, Bing wins Miss Wyman away from Mr. Tone.

This is perhaps Crosby's most enjoyable screen vehicle since *A Connecticut Yankee in King Arthur's Court* and remains the only lightweight Crosby film produced after 1950 that rekindled some of the charm and spirit of the performer's earlier motion pictures. Like *Going My Way* and *The Bells of St. Mary's*, two of Crosby's best and most well-remembered films, *Here Comes the Groom* is a well-constructed screen comedy that wisely presents its characters as real, three-dimensional people, rather than comic cardboard cutouts. As a result, it manages to touch the audience's spirit as well as its funnybone. This is almost entirely because of Frank Capra's sensitive and intelligent handling and the nicely balanced performances of Crosby, Jane Wyman, Franchot Tone, Alexis Smith, and Jacky Gencel.

Here Comes the Groom was a definite improvement over both *Top o' the Morning* and *Mr. Music*. This is the film in which the Groaner sang one of his bounciest movie tunes, "In the Cool, Cool, Cool of the Evening," which won the Academy Award as the best song for 1951. A brief clip from the picture, showing Crosby and Jane Wyman singing this song, was recently included in a television special.

195

With Jane Wyman

With Ethel Barrymore

Just for You

1952

CAST

Jordan Blake (BING CROSBY); Carolina Hill (JANE WYMAN); Alida De Bronkhart (*Ethel* BARRYMORE); Jerry Blake (*Robert Arthur*); Barbara Blake (*Natalie Wood*); Mrs. Angevine (*Cora Witherspoon*); Mr. Hodges (*Regis Toomey*); Georgie Polansky (*Ben Lessy*); Leo (*Art Smith*); Hank (*Willis Bouchey*); George (*Herbert Vigram*).

CREDITS

A Paramount Picture. Directed by Elliot Nugent. Produced by Pat Duggan. Screenplay by Robert Carson. Based on the Work "Famous," by Stephen Vincent Benet. Director of Photography: George Barnes, A.S.C. Filmed in Technicolor. Film Editor: Ellsworth Hoagland. Costumes by Edith Head. Musical Director: Emil Newman. Songs by Harry Warren and Leo Robin.

SONGS

"Zing a Little Zong"
"He's Just Crazy for Me"
"Just for You"
"The Live Oak Tree"
"A Flight of Fancy"
"I'll Si-Si Ya in Bahia"
"On the 10:10, (From Ten-Ten-Tennessee)"

Running Time: 95 minutes

With Robert Arthur

With Ben Lessy

Just for You is a minor film that reteams Bing Crosby and Jane Wyman in the story of a successful Broadway producer who feels that he has been less than successful as a parent. To alleviate his guilt, the producer (Crosby) rearranges his busy schedule so that he can spend more time with his neglected teenage son (Robert Arthur) and daughter (Natalie Wood).

Crosby decides to take them on an extended vacation at a country resort. Once there, however, he finds that he still has difficulty communicating with them and that he will need some help from his lovely and tactful fiancée (Jane Wyman). Bing sends for her, and upon her arrival she succeeds in easing some of the children's tension by explaining to them that their father has decided to decrease his show-business activities to become more of a family man again.

Further complications develop, however, when young Robert confesses to Jane that he has developed a crush on her and has written a love song

about her entitled "Just for You." Although Jane doesn't quite know how to react, she shows the song to Bing, who is so impressed with it that he begins making arrangements to have it published.

This does nothing to ease young Robert's heartache, and he decides to get away from it all by enlisting in the air force. As the months pass, Bing becomes concerned about his son's welfare and begins entertaining at various military installations in the hope of being reunited with him. At one military base, Bing locates his son and is pleased to discover that the lad has developed into a mature man and forgotten his adolescent crush.

Just for You contains no memorable songs, and Elliot Nugent's direction lacks the style and conviction that he has always been able to bring to a worthier vehicle. By the same token, Bing Crosby and Jane Wyman seemed to have a good time in their roles, but it was easy to see that neither performer really thought much of the project.

Road to Bali

1952

CAST

George Cochran (BING CROSBY); Harold Gridley (BOB HOPE); Lalah (DOROTHY LAMOUR); Len Arok (*Murvyn Vye*); Gung (*Peter Coe*); Bhoma Da (*Ralph Moody*); Ramayana (*Leon Askin*); Clerk (*Donald Lawton*); Lalah at seven (*Bunny Lewbel*); Guard (*Michael Ansara*); Dancer (*Jack Claus*); Bo Kassar (*Bernie Gozier*); Priest (*Herman Cantor*); Attendant (*Larry Chance*); Eunice (*Carolyn Jones*); Verna (*Jan Kayne*); Himself (*Bob Crosby*).

CREDITS

A Paramount Picture. Directed by Hal Walker. Produced by Harry Tugend. Screenplay by Frank Butler, Hal Kanter, and William Morrow. Director of Photography: George Barnes, A.S.C. Art Direction: Hal Pereira and Joseph McMillan Johnson. Set Decoration: Sam Comer and Russ Dowd. Film Editor: Archie Marshek. Sound Recording by Gene Merritt and John Cope. Musical Direction: Joseph J. Lilley. Musical Numbers Staged by Charles O'Curran. Orchestral Arrangements: Van Cleave. New Songs by James Van Heusen and Johnny Burke.

SONGS

"The Merry Go Runaround"
"Chicago Style"
"Hoot-Mon"
"To See You"
"Moonflowers"

Running Time: 90 minutes

With Dorothy Lamour and Bob Hope

Road to Bali is a colorful but basically disappointing *Road* adventure that fails in its attempt to re-create the marvelously insane humor that had become synonymous with most of the earlier entries in the series. The film contains a few hilarious comical interludes and some ridiculous and obvious Hollywood "in" jokes, but it emerges as a below-par *Road* picture.

Whereas the in jokes in the previous films had had the appearance of marvelous examples of creative ad-libbing, most of the ones in *Road to Bali* seem too contrived and outrageous to be convincing. Lacking the basic plot continuity that had served as a much-needed counterbalance for the zaniness in the earlier *Road* films, *Road to Bali* forces Bob and Bing to spend most of their screen time tossing off a huge variety of nonsensical jokes such as the sequence wherein the boys arrive at Bali and joyously ogle a shapely parade of luscious native maidens, when all of a sudden they hear an agonized groan coming from somewhere off screen. "What was that?" asks Crosby. Hope replies, "It's Errol Flynn. He can't stand it."

Road to Bali contains some lush technicolor photography (by *Emperor Waltz* alumnus George Barnes) and some convincing tropical scenic designs, but even these can do nothing to make the film more than an average screen comedy.

With Dorothy Lamour, Bob Hope and "Friend"

With Nicole Maurey

Little Boy Lost

1953

CAST

Bill Wainwright (BING CROSBY); Pierre Verdier (*Claude* DAUPHIN); Jean (The Little Boy) (*Christian Fourcade*); Mother Superior (*Gabrielle Dorziat*); Lisa Garret (*Nicole Maurey*); Nelly (*Colette Dereal*); Madame Quilleboeuf (*Georgette Anys*); Lt. Walker (*Peter Baldwin*); Helene (*Gladys de Segonzac*); Dr. Biroux (*Jean Del Val*); Nurse (*Adele St. Maur*); Suzanne Pitou (*Ninon Stratly*); Paul (*Jacques Gallo*); Stewardess (*Karin Vengay*); Sister Therese (*Tina Blagoi*); Waiter (*Arthur Dulac*).

CREDITS

A Paramount Picture. Directed by George Seaton. Produced by William Perlberg. Director of Photography: George Barnes, A.S.C. Art Direction: Hal Pereira and Henry Bumstead. Set Decoration: Sam Comer and Ross Dowd. Film Editor: Alma Macrorie. Screenplay by George Seaton. Based on the Story by Marghanita Laski. Sound Recording by Harry Mills and Gene Garvin. Musical Score: Victor Young. Costumes by Edith Head. New Songs by James Van Heusen and Johnny Burke.

Running Time: 95 minutes

With Christian Fourcade

In *Little Boy Lost,* Crosby appears as Bill Wainwright, a former war correspondent who had been on permanent assignment in Paris during the Nazi invasion. During his stay in Paris, he had married a beautiful member of the French resistance movement who was killed when her affiliation with the Underground was discovered. It is now several years after the war, and Wainwright has returned to Paris hoping to find his young son, Jean, lost during a bombing raid but believed to be still living in a Paris orphanage.

Arriving at the orphanage, Wainwright is introduced to an eight-year-old war orphan (Christian Fourcade) who may or may not be Wainwright's son. Although the child resembles his late wife, Wainwright wants to be certain beyond a doubt that the little fellow is his son. He takes the lad to the apartment where he and his wife had lived during the war. Once there, Bill asks the youngster if he remembers anything about the surroundings or about the beautiful woman who used to sing him to sleep. Much to Bill's disappointment, the child has no solid recollection of his mother, and the apartment is completely unfamiliar to him.

Several days later, however, the boy begins to remember certain pertinent details. He tells Bill that he now recalls the apartment, his beautiful mother, and even the little shop across the street. But Bill does not rejoice. He knows that the store across the street is a recent addition to the neighborhood. If the boy had been telling the truth, he wouldn't have had any recollection of it. Bill makes inquiries at the neighborhood shops and discovers that the boy was goaded into lying by a matronly laundress. Wainwright visits the woman and asks her why she told the child to lie. Resenting Bill's question, the woman tells him that she would do almost anything to give one of the orphans an opportunity for a better life.

Bill is now faced with a painful emotional dilemma. He feels affection toward the boy and would like very much to adopt him, but his strong, almost neurotic attachment to his late wife prevents him from fully loving a child who is not the product of their marriage. Bill decides to take the youngster back to the orphanage and subsequently makes arrangements to leave Paris.

He returns to his apartment where he is visited by his long-time friend Pierre Verdier (Claude Dauphin). Seeing that Wainwright is sad and disillusioned, Verdier asks him why he has decided not to adopt the boy. Bill regretfully explains that he cannot bring himself to accept the child and that it would be best for the youngster to remain at the orphanage. But Verdier, who also lost his wife during the war, begs Bill to bury the memory of his dead wife and to open his heart to the little boy. Moved by his friend's words, Wainwright returns to the orphanage.

Filmed almost entirely in Paris, *Little Boy Lost* is a film of dramatic impact. Its overall quality is partially due to the sensitive direction of George Seaton, who transformed an eight-year-old movie novice (the angelic Christian Fourcade) into a competent and highly expressive actor. Under Seaton's watchful guidance, the youngster handles his difficult, demanding role with all the proficiency of a well-seasoned professional. His performance exudes a strong emotional quality that belies both his youth and his inexperience. The child is matched every step of the way by Crosby's powerful portrayal of the protagonist. Crosby skillfully embroiders the role of a lonely man who has become saturated with painful uncertainties, unable to bury his mournful memories of the war and equally powerless to face squarely an uncertain future.

With Claude Dauphine and Georgette Anys

White Christmas

1954

CAST

Bob Wallace (BING CROSBY); Phil Davis (DANNY KAYE); Betty (*Rosemary* CLOONEY); Judy (*Vera* ELLEN); General Waverly (*Dean* JAGGER); Joe (*John Brascia*); Emma (*Mary Wickes*); Adjutant (*Richard Shannon*); Susan (*Anne Whitfield*); General's Guest (*Grady Sutton*); Landlord (*Sig Rumann*); Albert (*Robert Crosson*); Ed Harrison (*Johnny Grant*); Conductor (*Percy Helton*); General Carlton (*Gavin Gordon*).

CREDITS

A Paramount Picture. Directed by Michael Curtiz. Produced by Robert Emmett Dolan. Screenplay by Norman Panama, Melvin Frank, and Norman Krasna. Director of Photography: Loyal Griggs, A.S.C. In Technicolor. Also the First Motion Picture Filmed in VistaVision. Art Direction: Hal Pereira and Roland Anderson. Set Decoration: Sam Comer and Grace Gregory. Sound Recording by Hugo Grenzbach and John Cope. Film Editor: Frank Bracht. Costumes by Edith Head. Music and Lyrics by Irving Berlin. Musical Direction by Joseph J. Lilley. Dance Direction: Robert Alton.

SONGS

"Love, You Didn't Do Right by Me"
"White Christmas"
"Count Your Blessings"
"Sisters"
"The Old Man"

Running Time: 120 minutes

With Danny Kaye and Dean Jagger

With Rosemary Clooney

With Danny Kaye

With Danny Kaye

White Christmas is a curiously disappointing film. A glossy and colorful entertainment in which Bing Crosby and Danny Kaye are allowed to cavort amid some of Irving Berlin's most spirited show tunes, the film is vaguely reminiscent of the earlier Paramount offering *Holiday Inn,* in which Crosby and Fred Astaire were teamed together in a similar story. This resemblance is merely on the surface, though, and whereas *Holiday Inn* was one of Hollywood's brightest and most enjoyable musicals, *White Christmas* is remembered for its theme song and for very little else.

The threadbare story of *White Christmas* focused on the adventures of two talented song-and-dance men who came together while on active duty during the Second World War. When they are discharged, Crosby and Kaye become one of the hottest acts in show business and soon begin to expand their horizons by producing and directing their own shows, as well as starring in them. After five years of steady performing, Bing and Danny decide to take a little time off and go on vacation. Before they leave, they become involved with a pair of female entertainers (Rosemary Clooney and Vera Ellen) and soon find themselves accompanying the girls on a trip to a posh New England mountain resort. Arriving at the resort, the boys discover that the place has been doing terrible business and that its owner is on the verge of bankruptcy. Once Crosby and Kaye learn that the owner (Dean Jagger) is an old army chum of theirs, they decide to help him out by staging a huge benefit show at the resort. The ensuing show is, of course, a tremendous success, and the final scene finds Bing ending up with Rosemary and Danny in the arms of Vera.

The best thing about *White Christmas* is that it is a technically flawless picture. But no amount of technical virtuosity can negate the fact that the film should have been much better. Actually amounting to little more than an impressive succession of stunning visual images punctuated from time to time by an Irving Berlin song, *White Christmas* resembles *Blue Skies* in appearance, just as it resembles *Holiday Inn* in plot, but it fails to project the charm and appeal of either of the Berlin-Crosby vehicles that preceded it. Although *White Christmas* contains a few nice Technicolor visuals, the picture is really little more than a big, overblown Hollywood project that failed to live up to its expectations.

With Rosemary Clooney, Vera Ellen and Danny Kaye

With William Holden

The Country Girl

1954

CAST

Frank Elgin (BING CROSBY); Georgie Elgin (GRACE KELLY); Bernie Dodd (WILLIAM HOLDEN); Phil Cook (*Anthony Ross*); Larry (*Gene Reynolds*); Singer-Actress (*Jacqueline Fontaine*); Ed (*Eddie Ryder*); Paul Unger (*Robert Kent*); Henry Johnson (*John W. Reynolds*); First Woman (*Ida Moore*); Bartender (*Frank Scanell*); Second Woman (*Ruth Rickaby*); Actor (*Howard Joslin*); Actor (*Hal K. Dawson*); Photographer (*Charles Tannen*); Johnnie (*Jon Provost*); Bellboy (*Bob Alden*); Ralph (*Chester Jones*).

CREDITS

A Paramount Picture. Directed by George Seaton. A George Seaton—William Perlberg Production. Screenplay by George Seaton. From the Play by Clifford Odets. Director of Photography: John F. Warren, A.S.C. Art Direction: Hal Pereira and Roland Anderson. Set Decoration: Sam Comer and Grace Gregory. Musical Score by Victor Young. Sound Recording by Gene Merritt and John Cope. Costumes by Edith Head. Film Editor: Ellsworth Hoagland. Musical Numbers Staged by Robert Alton. Songs by Ira Gershwin and Harold Arlen.

SONGS

"The Pitchman"
"Live and Learn"
"The Search Is Through"

Running Time: 104 minutes

With Grace Kelly and William Holden

With Grace Kelly

The Country Girl is Bing Crosby's most famous dramatic film and one in which he delivers a powerful performance. Based on a successful play that tells of an alcoholic stage actor given a chance for a comeback by a brash young director, the film presents Crosby with a role similar to the character of the war correspondent Bill Wainwright in *Little Boy Lost* but on a much larger scale. Whereas Wainwright was an unhappy but basically uncomplicated man, the character of actor Frank Elgin in *The Country Girl* is extremely complex, requiring an actor to show the many different sides of a man who can be kind, cruel, loving, frightened, and neurotic.

George Seaton's film is an excellent example of how a stage play should be filmed. It is also a superb illustration of how extraordinary Crosby's range and versatility as a performer actually are. In the difficult role of the alcoholic actor Frank Elgin, Crosby is able to completely submerge his own buoyant personality beneath a tortured mask of alcoholic despair and insecurity.

The Country Girl opens as the washed-up stage star shows up late to audition for the leading role in a musical play that will be directed by a tough but accomplished young stage director, Bernie Dodd (William Holden). Dodd was once one of Elgin's biggest fans, and now he wants to give the actor a chance for a comeback, casting him as the lead in the play.

Although Dodd has a great deal of confidence in Elgin's ability to stay off the bottle, Frank does not share Bernie's enthusiasm. Elgin has never been able to regain his nerve ever since he inadvertently caused the death of his young son, Johnnie. As a result, Elgin spends most of his time drinking and reminiscing about the happy times before his son's death.

Realizing that Elgin's frame of mind is unhealthy, Dodd visits Elgin at home, where he meets Frank's

With Jacqueline Fontaine

With (left to right) producer William Perlberg, director George Seaton, cameraman John W. Warren, Grace Kelly and William Holden

strong-willed wife, Georgie (Grace Kelly). Dodd begins to get the impression that Georgie is really the cause of Elgin's turmoil, and he takes steps to keep her away from Frank during the subsequent rehearsals.

Learning of this, Elgin begs Dodd to let Georgie stay on, because she is very unstable and might commit suicide if separated from Frank for any length of time. Giving in to Frank's wishes, but angrily, Dodd begins to have some fierce encounters with Georgie, telling her that she is a burden to Frank and that she is holding him back from climbing back to the top of his profession. Furious at Dodd's accusations, Georgie tells Dodd to keep his nose out of something he really doesn't understand.

A few days before the play is scheduled to open, Frank shatters Bernie's faith in him by taking off on a major binge and winding up in the police drunk tank. After drying Elgin out, the authorities turn him over to Georgie and Dodd, who have since further complicated matters by becoming romantically involved. During this time, Dodd has learned that Georgie is actually Elgin's driving force and that Frank is really the unstable partner in the marriage. With a tremendous amount of coaching from

Bernie, Elgin manages to perform brilliantly in the play and thus win back the confidence he had formerly had. At a small celebration after the performance, Elgin senses that Bernie and Georgie have become involved with each other. However, Georgie sees that Frank has become a new man as a result of his success in the play, and she decides to stay with him.

The Country Girl is an acting tour-de-force for Crosby, Grace Kelly, and William Holden. For Miss Kelly, the role of Georgie provides a welcome opportunity to rise above her "aloof society girl" screen image and prove to both audiences and critics that there was considerably more to her talent than charm and beauty. William Holden's role as the chain-smoking young director was likewise a pivotal role that helped put his boy-next-door image to rest. It was largely responsible for the tremendous screen success Holden afterward enjoyed. The part of Frank Elgin is probably the meatiest role Crosby has played. His Frank Elgin is a larger-than-life study of a pitiful, beaten man who has lost everything worthwhile to him and is reduced to a weary, drunken shadow of his former self. It is a shattering, realistic, and masterful screen portrait.

With William Holden and Grace Kelly

With Jeanmarie, Mitzi Gaynor and Donald O'Connor

Anything Goes

1956

CAST

Bill Benson (BING CROSBY); Ted Adams (DONALD O'CONNOR); Patsy Blair (*Mitzi Gaynor*); Gaby Duval (*Jeanmaire*); Steve Blair (*Phil Harris*); Victor Lawrence (*Kurt Kasznar*); Alex Todd (*Walter Sande*); Ed Brent (*Richard Erdman*); Suzanne (*Argentina Brunetti*); Otto (*Archer MacDonald*); French Baroness (*Alma Macrorie*); Paul Holiday (*James Griffith*).

CREDITS

A Paramount Picture. Directed by Robert Lewis. Produced by Robert Emmett Dolan. Screenplay by Sidney Sheldon. Based on the Play by P. G. Wodehouse and Guy Bolton. Revised by Russell Crouse and Howard Lindsay. Director of Photography: John F. Warren, A.S.C. Film Editor: Frank Bracht. Music Arranged and Conducted by Joseph J. Lilley. Orchestral Arrangements by Van Cleave Choreography by Nick Castle. Filmed in Technicolor and VistaVision. Title Dance Direction: Ernie Platt. Ballet Direction: Roland Petit. New Songs by James Van Heusen and Sammy Cahn.

SONG

"I Get a Kick Out of You"
"You're the Top"
"All Through the Night"
"It's De-Lovely"
"You Can Bounce Right Back"

Running Time: 106 minutes

With Donald O'Connor

Produced in 1956, *Anything Goes* reunited Crosby with Donald O'Connor almost twenty years after their successful collaboration in *Sing You Sinners*. The picture was also Crosby's second film adaptation of the Cole Porter Broadway hit. The first version was a faithful but stilted approach to the lively musical play. The second version jettisoned the original plot and substituted an even weaker storyline. Most of the lilting Porter music was retained.

In this treatment, Crosby and O'Connor are cast in the familiar roles of show-business stars who, planning a mammoth musical entertainment, travel around the world in a search of an appropriate feminine lead.

The stars, along with Renée Jeanmaire and Mitzi Gaynor, perform with animated spirit, and Robert Lewis's direction is competent enough. Eventually, however, all are defeated by the trite screenplay and the economical production values Paramount provided.

Anything Goes was Bing's last Paramount film, a weak farewell to a relationship that had provided him with some of his most impressive vehicles. Happily, his next picture (his second for MGM) provided Crosby with one of the best roles and some of the best material his long career had enjoyed. And it gave him Frank Sinatra as a co-star.

High Society

1956

CAST

C. K. Dexter-Haven (BING CROSBY); Tracy Lord (GRACE KELLY); Mike Connor (FRANK SINATRA); Liz (*Celeste* HOLM); Uncle Willie (*Louis* CALHERN); George (*John Lund*); Seth Lord (*Sidney Blackmer*); Mrs. Lord (*Margalo Gillmore*); Caroline (*Lydia Reed*); Mac (*Richard Keene*); Parson (*Hugh Boswell*); Himself (LOUIS ARMSTRONG).

CREDITS

A Metro-Goldwyn-Mayer Picture. Directed by Charles Walters. Produced by Sol C. Siegel. Screenplay by John Patrick. Based on the Play by Philip Barry. Director of Photography: Paul C. Vogel. Art Direction: Cedric Gibbons and Hans Peters. Set Decoration: Richard Pefferle and Edwin Willis. Film Editor: Ralph E. Winters. Sound Recording: Wesley Miller. Filmed in Technicolor. Costumes by Helen Rose. Makeup by William Tuttle. Songs by Cole Porter.

SONGS

"Now You Has Jazz"
"Mind If I Make Love to You"
"True Love"
"High Society"
"Well, Did You Evah?"
"I Love You, Samantha"

Running Time: 107 minutes

With Louis Armstrong

With Frank Sinatra

With Grace Kelly and Louis Calhern

With John Lund, Grace Kelly and Frank Sinatra

A lighthearted musical remake of Phillip Barry's *The Philadelphia Story* that seemed to delight everyone, *High Society* cast Grace Kelly as a young society matron who is about to marry a pompous society chap played by John Lund. Back into Miss Kelly's life, however, comes her estranged husband (Bing Crosby), who believes that her marriage to Lund is a foolish mistake that will make her miserable. Also entering the scene are a laconic young reporter (Frank Sinatra) and his female assistant (Celeste Holm), assigned to do an elaborate layout for a major magazine on Miss Kelly's wedding. Everything proceeds according to schedule until Miss Kelly begins to harbor second thoughts of her own about marrying Lund. These doubts are reflected by a brief moonlight fling with reporter Sinatra. Eventually, though, her former hubby, Crosby, wins Grace back once and for all.

Miss Kelly is bright and vivacious as the young socialite with romantic troubles. Crosby and Sinatra glide through the film with complete ease as the two fellows who try to win Grace away from Lund. But the brisk and tuneful repertoire of songs and the polished production techniques are what prevent *High Society* from becoming another of those star-studded but standard musical extravaganzas that were so popular during the early and middle fifties. Although Crosby handles his vocal assignments in his usual superb manner, Frank Sinatra's rendition of "Mind If I Make Love to You" stands as the musical highlight. This arrangement allowed Sinatra to display his ability to bring a definite dramatic interpretation to almost every song he sings.

High Society was extremely successful at the time of its release and has enjoyed great popularity during its many showings on television.

With Malcolm Broderick and Inger Stevens

Man on Fire presents Crosby as middle-aged Earl Carleton, whose business life has been a great triumph but whose personal life has been unsuccessful. As the film opens, Carleton's wife, Gwen (Mary Fickett), has divorced him and married an amiable but self-righteous chap named Bryan Seward (Richard Eastham). The split was unfriendly, and Carleton has become angry and embittered over the divorce. He has even gone so far as to prevent his ex-wife from seeing their only child, Ted (Malcolm Broderick). Although Carleton's friends Nina Wylie (Inger Stevens) and Sam Dunstock (E. G. Marshall) have both begged the stubborn businessman to be more reasonable, Carleton insists upon keeping his son to himself, regardless of who gets hurt.

Carleton and his boy are soon brought before Judge Randolph (Anne Seymour) to find a solution. After speaking to young Ted, the judge decides to reject Carleton's request for total custody and orders that the child be turned over to Gwen and her new husband. Angered and hurt, Carleton attempts to take his son by force, but he soon realizes his faults and comes to his senses.

One of the better films of the soap-opera school, *Man on Fire* is a taut and low-keyed drama that makes the most of its budget and its production values. Inger Stevens and E. G. Marshall are both excellent as Crosby's faithful friends who attempt to bring the embittered businessman back to his senses. Stevens in particular proves, in her compassionate scenes with Crosby, that she was a vastly underrated actress capable of much better roles than she was usually given. In the role of Earl Carleton, Crosby weaves a superb portrayal of a strange and paradoxical man. Again demonstrating his skill and range, Crosby performs on a variety of levels throughout the film. He is enormously successful in showing both the good and the bad sides of the character. A scene that illustrates this is that in which Crosby meets his wife's new husband and says, "You know, you're not such a bad guy after all. I might even be able to like you under different circumstances."

Say One for Me

1959

CAST

Father Conroy (BING CROSBY); Holly (*Debbie Reynolds*); Tony Vincent (*Robert Wagner*); Phil Stanley (*Ray Walston*); Harry LaMaise (*Les Tremayne*); Jim Dugan (*Frank McHugh*); Joe (*Joe Besser*); Chorine (*Stella Stevens*); Fay Flagg (*Connie Gilchrist*); Monsignor (*Sebastian Cabot*); Dr. Leventhal (*Thomas B. Henry*); Rabbi Berman (*David Leonard*); June January (*Judy Harriet*); Otto (*Murray Alper*); Captain Bradford (*Richard Collier*).

CREDITS

A 20th Century-Fox Picture. Produced and Directed by Frank Tashlin. Screenplay By Robert O'Brien. Director of Photography: Leo Tover, A.S.C. Art Direction: Lyle R. Wheeler and Leland Fuller. Set Decoration: Walter M. Scott and Eli Benneche. Film Editor: Hugh S. Fowler. Sound Recording: E. Clayton Ward and Harry M. Leonard. Costume Design: Adele Palmer. Music Supervised and Conducted by Lionel Newman. Dance Direction: Alex Romero. Assistant Director: Joseph E. Rickards. Vocal Supervision: Charles Henderson. Filmed In CinemaScope. Color By Deluxe. Songs by James Van Heusen and Sammy Cahn.

Running Time: 119 minutes

With Debbie Reynolds

With Robert Wagner

In spite of his matchless popularity as a musical-comedy star, Bing Crosby is perhaps best remembered for his portrayal of Father Chuck O'Malley in *Going My Way* and *The Bells of St. Mary's*. Crosby has perhaps become almost every moviegoer's ideal screen priest; he brought marvelous warmth, tenderness, and humanity to his protrayals of a man of the cloth. As a result, Bing Crosby was once again cast as a priest in a handsomely produced but overlong and monotonous picture entitled *Say One for Me*.

Despite a fairly original plotline featuring Bing as an easygoing middle-aged clergyman who runs a church catering to show people, and a fairly interesting romantic subplot revolving around Debbie Reynolds and Robert Wagner, *Say One for Me* is pretty dull. The film is slow moving and tends to waste good talent (such as Ray Walston and Frank McHugh) in unworthy red-herring roles. Moreover, the use of a glossy but shallow and one-dimensional color process (known as "Deluxe") makes the picture look pale when one compares it with Technicolor. It must be admitted, however, that the Bingle is allowed to make the most of his third appearance as a priest, and he makes the character into just the kind of down-to-earth middle-aged clergyman Father O'Malley might well have become once he passed age fifty.

High Time
1960

CAST

Harvey Howard (BING CROSBY); Gil Sparrow (FABIAN); Joy Elder (*Tuesday* WELD); Helene Gauthier (*Nicole Maurey*); Bob Bannerman (*Richard Beymer*); Randy Pruitt (*Yvonne Craig*); T. J. (*Patrick Adiarte*); Higgson (*Jimmy Boyd*); President (*Kenneth MacKenna*); Thayer (*Gavin MacLeod*); Laura (*Nina Shipman*); Harvey Howard, Jr. (*Angus Duncan*); Crump (*Paul Schreiber*); Bones McKinney (*Dick Crockett*).

CREDITS

A 20th Century-Fox Picture. Directed by Blake Edwards. Produced by Charles Brackett. A Bing Crosby Production. Screenplay by Tom and Frank Waldman. Based on a Story by Garson Kanin. Director of Photography: Ellsworth Fredericks. Art Direction: Herman A. Blumenthal and Duncan Cramer. Film Editor: Robert Simpson. Filmed in Color by Deluxe. Musical Score by Henry Mancini. Songs by Sammy Cahn and James Van Heusen.

Running Time: 102 minutes

One of the best of Crosby's later motion pictures, *High Time* is the amusing story of a wealthy middle-aged widower, Harvey Howard (Bing Crosby), who decides to acquire the college education he never had. Although both his grown children think Harvey's idea is foolish, he is determined to get his four years of higher education, no matter what. On admission day, Harvey tells the university officials that he does not want any special treatment because of his age; he would rather be looked upon as just another freshman.

Soon the aging freshman finds himself going through an embarassing initiation ritual to become a member of a fraternity. For this initiation Harvey must dress up as an elderly dowager and attend a fancy ball. After his initiation, Harvey is admitted to the fraternity.

Meanwhile, Harvey finds himself attracted to a pretty French professor named Helene Gauthier (Nicole Maurey). Although she reciprocates his affection, Harvey tells her that he could probably sprout wings and fly more easily than he could remarry. On graduation day, Harvey makes a speech in front of the student body and concludes by saying, "I could no more get married again than I could fly." Then he is lifted off the ground by invisible wires and begins flying around the auditorium.

High Time is pure nonsense from beginning to end, but the lighthearted attitude of Bing Crosby, Nicole Maurey, and their young co-stars makes it better than one might expect. Crosby is very good as the student, and he is given able support by a spirited young cast including Fabian, Tuesday Weld, Richard Beymer, and Yvonne Craig. Although Crosby's role is relatively straight acting, the venerable crooner was given the opportunity to sing one of the nicest love songs of the sixties, "The Second Time Around."

With Tuesday Weld and Richard Beymer

With Joan Collins and Bob Hope

With Dorothy Lamour and Bob Hope

The Road to Hong Kong

1962

CAST

Harry Turner, (BING CROSBY); Chester Babcock (BOB HOPE); Diane (JOAN COLLINS); Dorothy Lamour (DOROTHY LAMOUR); Leader (*Robert* MORLEY); High Lama (*Felix Aylmer*); Jhinnah (*Roger Delgardo*); Dr. Zorbb (*Walter Gotell*); Lama (*Peter Madden*); American Officials (*Robert Ayres, Alan Gifford, Robin Hughes*); Agent (*Bill Nagy*); Photographer (*Guy Standeven*); Messenger (*John McCarthy*); Servant (*Simon Levy*); Chinese Girl (*Mei Ling*); Receptionist (*Katya Douglas*); Special Guest Stars (FRANK SINATRA, DEAN MARTIN, DAVID NIVEN, PETER SELLERS, JERRY COLONNA).

CREDITS

A Melnor Picture released through United Artists. Directed by Norman Panama. Produced by Melvin Frank. Original Screenplay by Norman Panama and Melvin Frank. Director of Photography: Jack Hildyard, B.S.C. Art Direction: Sydney Cain and Bill Hutchinson. Set Dresser: Maurice Fowler. Film Editor: John Smith. Sound: A. G. Ambler and Red Law. Sound Editor: Chris Greenham. Assistant Director: Bluey Hill. Production Designer: Roger Furse. Make up by Dave Aylott. Special Effects by Wally Veevers and Ted Samuels. Animation by Biographic Cartoon Films, Ltd. Main Title Designed by Maurice Bender. Music by Robert Farnon. Songs by Sammy Cahn and James Van Heusen.

SONGS

"Let's Not Be Sensible"
"Teamwork"
"It's the Only Way to Travel"
"We're on the Road to Hong Kong"
"Warmer Than a Whisper"

Running Time: 91 minutes

With Bob Hope and Peter Sellers

The Road to Hong Kong cannot really be called a genuine entry in the Road series. It is actually only a mildly amusing international romp in which Bing and Bob make a valiant attempt to recapture the wonderful craziness and uninhibited spirit of the earlier films in the series. The film was one of the top-grossing motion pictures released during 1962, but it bears little resemblance to any of the "bona fide" Road adventures and lacks their general hilarity. The film emerges as an understandable disappointment to filmgoers who recall the superb comic effectiveness of most of the earlier entries.

The Road to Hong Kong finds Bob suffering from amnesia. Bing takes him to a high lama in Tibet, to restore Hope's memory. The lama is so successful that Bob develops total recall. As a result,

he becomes the prime target for a group of international spies planning to take control of the universe.

Forced to flee to Hong Kong, Bob and Bing run across their old pal Dorothy Lamour (appearing as herself) and ask her to help them out of their jam. Always willing to lend a hand, Dorothy gives the boys a shot in her new nightclub routine, hoping to throw the spies off the track. Finally, however, Bob and Bing are flown via spaceship to a far-off asteroid, where they meet unlikely spacemen Frank Sinatra and Dean Martin.

The Road to Hong Kong is the only Road film that wasn't made in Hollywood. Produced not by Paramount, but by Melnor Films, Ltd., in conjunction with United Artists, it was filmed at England's Shepperton Studios in Middlesex.

Robin and the 7 Hoods

1964

CAST

Robbo (FRANK SINATRA); John (DEAN MARTIN); Will (SAMMY DAVIS, JR.); Allen A. Dale (BING CROSBY); Guy Gisbourne (Peter FALK); Marian (*Barbara Rush*); Crocker (*Victor Buono*); Police Chief (*Barry Kelley*); Six Second (*Hank Henry*); Blue Jaw (*Robert Carricart*); Vermin (*Allen Jenkins*); Tomatoes (*Jack La Rue*); Mr. Ricks (*Hans Conreid*); Hammacher (*Sig Rumann*); Sheriff Glick (*Robert Foulk*); Gimp (*Phil Arnold*); Soup Meat (*Harry Swoger*); Tick (*Joseph Ruskin*); Liver Jackson (*Bernard Fein*); The Hoods (*Sonny King, Phil Crosby, Richard Bakalyan*); Judge (*Milton Rudin*); Dignitary (*Maurice Manson*).

CREDITS

A Warner Brothers Picture. Directed by Gordon Douglas. Produced by Frank Sinatra. Screenplay by David Schwartz. Director of Photography: William H. Daniels. Executive Producer: Howard W. Koch. Associate Producer: William H. Daniels. Art Direction: LeRoy Deane. Musical Score and Direction by Nelson Riddle. Orchestrations by Gil C. Grau. Film Editor: Sam O'Steen. Songs by Sammy Cahn and James Van Heusen.

SONGS

"Style"
"Mr. Booze"
"My Kind of Town"
"All for One and One for All"
"Charlotte Couldn't Charleston"
"Any Man Who Loves His Mother"
"Don't Be a Do-Badder"
"Bang-bang"

Running Time: 103 minutes

With Frank Sinatra and Dean Martin

Not really a Bing Crosby vehicle, *Robin and the 7 Hoods* features Frank Sinatra, Dean Martin, and Sammy Davis, Jr., in a lightly amusing "gangster" saga that modernizes the Robin Hood legend by substituting a group of Runyonesque Chicago gangsters for Robin and his merry men. What emerges on screen is a sluggish combination of some lively Hollywood talent attempting to coax laughs from routine material.

The film begins with the assassination of the most important gang leader in Chicago, Big Jim (Edward G. Robinson in an unbilled "guest" appearance). Following Big Jim's demise, the mobs of Guy Gisbourne (Peter Falk) and Robbo (Frank Sinatra) each try to gain control of the coveted North Side of Chicago, vandalizing each other's nightclubs during the rivalry.

Later, Robbo gains the public's favor when a mild-mannered orphanage worker, Allen A. Dale (Bing Crosby), begins publicizing Robbo as a kind of "Robin Hood" figure after Robbo's pal Will (Sammy Davis, Jr.) gives fifty thousand dollars to Dale's orphanage. The fifty grand was given to Robbo by Big Jim's lovely daughter Marian (Barbara Rush) because she wanted Robbo to take care of the gang that killed her father.

Marian uses another of Robbo's friends, John (Dean Martin), as her partner in a counterfeiting operation, using Robbo's newly formed charity interests as a convenient front. When Marian learns that Robbo has heard of her activities, she instructs Gisbourne to dispose of both Robbo and John, but Guy muffs his chance and finds himself encased in cement. Afterward, Marian organizes a women's crime-fighting brigade, which forces Robbo, John, and Will out of business. Later, Robbo and his two friends are astonished when they learn that Marian's newest "accomplice" is Allen A. Dale.

Although Crosby's part in *Robin and the 7 Hoods* is a supporting role, he is featured as the main attraction of one of the film's best musical numbers, "Mr. Booze." An obvious takeoff on one of *Guys and Dolls'* routines—"Sit Down, You're Rockin' the Boat"—"Mr. Booze" features Bing as the leader of a spirited revival meeting at which each of Robbo's gangsters "testifies" to the evils of drink. Crosby is also featured in an excellent song-and-dance routine with Frank Sinatra and Dean Martin, in addition to a catchy number entitled "Don't Be a Do-Badder," in which he tells the children at his orphanage to stay on the straight and narrow.

With Hank Henry, Dean Martin, Sammy Davis, Jr., Frank Sinatra, Richard Bakalyan and Phil Crosby

Stagecoach

1966

CAST

Dallas (ANN-MARGRET); Doc Boone (BING CROSBY); Mr. Peacock (RED BUTTONS); Ringo (ALEX CORD); Hatfield (MICHAEL CONNORS); Mr. Gatewood (BOB CUMMINGS); Curly (VAN HEFLIN); Buck (*Slim Pickens*); Lucy Mallory (*Stefanie Powers*); Luke Plummer (*Keenan Wynn*); Lt. Blanchard (*Joseph Hoover*); Captain Mallory (*John Gabriel*); Matt Plummer (*Brad Weston*); Mr. Haines (*Oliver McGowan*); Trooper (*Bruce Mars*); Sergeant (*Brett Pearson*).

CREDITS

A 20th Century-Fox Picture. Directed by Gordon Douglas. Produced by Martin Rackin. Associate Producer: Alvin G. Manuel. Screenplay by Joseph Landon. Based on the Original Screenplay by Dudley Nichols. From the Story by Ernest Haycox. Director of Photography: William H. Clothier. Assistant Director: Joseph E. Rickards. Filmed in CinemaScope. Color by Deluxe. Music by Jerry Goldsmith. Song: "Stagecoach To Cheyenne," by Paul Vance and Lee Pockriss. Sung by Wayne Newton. Portraits by Norman Rockwell.

Running Time: 114 minutes

With Ann-Margaret

With Van Heflin

With Ann-Margret

240

Attempting to remake the 1939 John Ford classic, *Stagecoach*, with any degree of success is foolhardy —tantamount to trying to redo *Citizen Kane, Gone with the Wind*, or *The Wizard of Oz*.

20th Century-Fox deserves credit for being brave enough to try and remake so widely acclaimed a motion picture. They did invest their *Stagecoach* remake with an all-star cast, lavish production values, and an atmospheric music score by Jerry Goldsmith. Regrettably, these elements do nothing to compensate for the film's lack of the pictorial beauty and character development that had made the original such a masterpiece. In fact, the 20th Century-Fox remake would probably have been a *total* failure had it not been for Crosby's portrayal of the drunken Doc Boone (played by Thomas Mitchell in the earlier film), who forces himself into sobriety to deliver the baby of a fellow stagecoach passenger.

Filmed almost thirty years after the earlier version, Fox's 1966 remake features the same plotline and characters. It begins as a diverse group of people accompany each other on a long and potentially dangerous cross-country stagecoach journey. These passengers include an outcast dance-hall queen, Dallas (Ann-Margret); an alcoholic doctor, Josiah Boone (Bing Crosby); a timid liquor dealer, constantly bothered by sinus trouble (Red Buttons); a suave Mississippi gambler (Michael Connors); a banker who has just embezzled from his own bank (Bob Cummings); and the pregnant wife of a Union-army officer (Stefanie Powers). Rounding out this colorful group are the stagecoach driver (Slim Pickens) and a gruff peace officer, Curly (Van Heflin).

During the journey, the group is joined by the Ringo Kid (Alex Cord), a hunted outlaw whom Curly promptly arrests. Later, Doc Boone uses a homemade emetic (a mixture of coal oil and salt) to sober himself up before successfully delivering the army wife's baby. Following a massive Indian attack, the stagecoach finally arrives at its destination.

It is interesting to compare the performance of Bing Crosby in this version of *Stagecoach* with that of the late Thomas Mitchell in the original version. Crosby opted to portray Doc Boone as a tragicomic drunkard, whereas Mitchell chose to play the part on a more serious level. In spite of their differing interpretations, however, each gives a superb performance in his own right.

I Surrender, Dear

Crosby Short Subjects, Cameos, Bit Parts

THE SHORT SUBJECTS

(The following list has been assembled from the limited data available. It is hoped that it is complete and accurate. For some of the films, supporting players have been documented along with the studio name and release date.)

1. **TWO PLUS FOURS** (Pathé 1930)

2. **I SURRENDER DEAR** (Mack Sennett, 1931)

3. **JUST ONE MORE CHANCE** (Mack Sennett, 1931)

4. **BILLBOARD GIRL** (Mack Sennett–Atlantic Pictures 1931), co-starring Franklin Pangborn and Babe Kane

5. **DREAMHOUSE** (Mack Sennett, 1931)

6. **BLUE OF THE NIGHT** (Mack Sennett, 1931), co-starring Franklin Pangborn and Babe Kane

7. **SING, BING, SING** (Mack Sennett–Paramount, 1931), co-starring Irving Bacon, Florine McKinney, and Franklin Pangborn

and Other Miscellaneous Film Appearances

8. **BRING ON BING** (Mack Sennett–Paramount, 1931)

9. **HOLLYWOOD ON PARADE** (Paramount, 1932), co-starring Gary Cooper and Stuart Erwin

10. **STAR NIGHT AT THE COCOANUT GROVE** (1935), also featuring Gary Cooper and Jack Oakie

11. **HOLLYWOOD VICTORY CARAVAN** (Paramount, 1945), with Humphrey Bogart, Bob Hope, Alan Ladd, and Barbara Stanwyck

display poster from Crosby short subject Sing, Bing, Sing

With the Brox Sisters, Al Rinker and Harry Barris in King of Jazz *(Universal, 1930)*

CAMEOS AND BIT PARTS

1. **KING OF JAZZ** (Universal, 1930). In this lavishly produced musical revue revolving around Paul Whiteman and his orchestra, Crosby and his fellow Rhythm Boys, Al Rinker and Harry Barris, appeared briefly with the Brox Sisters in a musical routine entitled "A Bench in the Park." *King of Jazz* also boasted an array of Academy Award–winning scenic designs by Universal's foremost art director, Herman Rosse (*Frankenstein* and *Dracula*). These included a stunning collection of gigantic pianos, outsized drums and bugles, and an eye-dazzling setting for the film's "Melting Pot" finale, which reminds the viewer of *The Wizard of Oz*."

2. **CHECK AND DOUBLE CHECK** (RKO, 1930). It has been said that Bing Crosby worked on this Amos 'n' Andy film (perhaps as a singer or a walk-on), but what Crosby had to do with this picture remains one of those curious Hollywood mysteries that will probably never be solved.

3. **REACHING FOR THE MOON** (United Artists, 1930). A mildly enjoyable and fast-moving entertainment featuring Douglas Fairbanks, Sr., Edward Everett Horton, and Bebe Daniels. *Reaching for the Moon* is most remembered for a brief interlude wherein an incredibly young and skinny Crosby sang "Low Down."

4. **CONFESSIONS OF A CO-ED** (Paramount Publix, 1931) Crosby's last "legitimate" bit part was in this ridiculous college drama, in which Sylvia Sidney, Phillips Holmes, Norman Foster and Claudia Dell appeared as four extremely adventurous university students who become involved in a series of campus scandals.

5. **THE BIG BROADCAST OF 1936** (Paramount, 1936). Under the direction of Norman Taurog, this was one of the best of the later *Big Broadcast* films, featuring such stalwarts as Burns and Allen, Jack Oakie, Lyda Roberti, and Bing Crosby doing a guest shot and rendering "I Wished on the Moon" and "Why Dream?"

6. **MY FAVORITE BLONDE** (Paramount, 1942, directed by Sidney Lanfield). The famous "feud" between Hope and Crosby had been started in 1940's *Road to Singapore* and become firmly established in *Road to Zanzibar*. As a result, Bing Crosby began making a series of cameo appearances in some of his partner's solo vehicles. In the first of these, Bob and Madeleine Carroll ask Crosby for directions during their flight from a gang of international cutthroats. A year later, in *Star Spangled Rhythm*, Bob spoke of Bing's guest shot in *My Favorite Blonde*, asking Betty Hutton, "Did you see that nice shot I gave

With Sylvia Sidney and Phillips Holmes in Confessions of a Co-ed

Crosby in *My Favorite Blonde*? You know, I like to throw all the work his way that I can, because those kids eat like horses."

7. **THE PRINCESS AND THE PIRATE** (Samuel Goldwyn, 1944; directed by David Butler). In this spoof of Hollywood pirate adventures, Bob Hope spends most of his screen time in pursuit of lovely Princess Virginia Mayo. During the picture's final five minutes, it looks as though Bob is finally going to get the princess, but at the last instant Crosby saunters in out of nowhere and takes Princess Virginia in his arms. Naturally chagrined, Hope looks directly into the camera and says with mock anger: "This is a fine thing! I knock my brains out for nine reels and then some bit player from Paramount comes on to grab all the goods. This is the last picture I do for Goldwyn!"

8. **DUFFY'S TAVERN** (Paramount, 1945; directed by Hal Walker). A poor film adaptation of the radio show, this little item is noted chiefly for featuring

practically the entire talent roster of Paramount Pictures in a variety of sketches and musical routines.

9. **OUT OF THIS WORLD** (Paramount, 1945; directed by Hal Walker). An occasionally funny spoof about the life of a popular singing idol, this almost-forgotten Hollywood film featured Eddie Bracken in the role of a Crosby-like crooner. Indeed, the voice synched in for Bracken in the film was that of the Groaner himself.

10. **VARIETY GIRL** (Paramount, 1947; directed by Hal Walker). In this lavishly produced but standard star-studded studio extravaganza, Bing Crosby and Bob Hope appeared as themselves in a clever golf sketch. Also appearing were Gary Cooper, Ray Milland, Alan Ladd, Paulette Goddard, Barbara Stanwyck, Dorothy Lamour, William Holden, Burt Lancaster, William Bendix, Robert Preston, Barry Fitzgerald, William Demarest, Billy De Wolfe, Veronica Lake, Patric Knowles, and Joan Caulfield. Despite the impressive cast, however, *Variety Girl* was a limp motion picture.

11. **MY FAVORITE BRUNETTE** (Paramount, 1947; directed by Elliot Nugent). One of the best and most entertaining of Bob Hope's spy spoofs, this comedy featured Bob as an affable baby photographer who gets involved with such veteran screen heavies as Peter Lorre, Lon Chaney, and Charles Dingle. The villains pin a false murder rap on Bob, and in the last five minutes of the picture, Hope is on his way to the gas chamber. At the last minute, however, heroine Dorothy Lamour produces evidence that vindicates Hope. The executioner turns out to be Bing, who storms off in a huff when he receives the news that Bob is a free man. In keeping with tradition, Bob looks at the camera and says, "Boy, he'll take any kind of a part."

Duffy's Tavern *(Paramount, 1945) with Jean Heather, Helen Walker and Gail Russell*

With Bob Hope in The Greatest Show on Earth *(Paramount, 1952)*

247

248
Showing his sons drawings for The Adventures
of Ichabod and Mr. Toad (*Walt Disney-RKO,
1949*)

With Bob Hope and William Demarest in Variety Girl.

12. **THE GREATEST SHOW ON EARTH** (Paramount, 1952; directed by Cecil B. DeMille). In this Oscar-winning spectacle dealing with life and love under a circus tent, Bing Crosby and Bob Hope were glimpsed briefly as a couple of interested onlookers during a circus performance.

13. **SON OF PALEFACE** (Paramount, 1952; directed by Frank Tashlin). Bob Hope and Jane Russell in an entertaining sequel to their earlier hit *The Paleface;* Crosby appears in another one of his amusing guest appearances in a Hope film.

14. **SCARED STIFF** (Paramount, 1953; directed by George Marshall). An often hilarious Dean Martin and Jerry Lewis vehicle highlighted by a surprise guest shot by Bing Crosby and Bob Hope.

15. **ALIAS JESSE JAMES** (United Artist–Hope Enterprises, Inc., 1959; directed by Norman Z. McLeod). One of the last of Bob Hope's better screen comedies, this hilarious farce contained surprise guest appearances by Bing Crosby, Gary Cooper, Gene Autry, Roy Rogers, and several television-Western stars including James (Matt Dillon) Arness, Hugh (Wyatt Earp) O'Brien, Ward (Major Adams) Bond, Gail (Annie Oakley) Davis, Jay (Tonto) Silverheels, and James (Maverick) Garner.

16. **LET'S MAKE LOVE** (20th Century-Fox, 1960; directed by George Cukor). A handsomely produced and glossy film starring Yves Montand and Marilyn Monroe and featuring nice guest shots by Bing Crosby, Gene Kelly, and Milton Berle.

17. **PEPE** (Columbia, 1960; directed by George Sidney). A spectacular failure, this star-studded "spectacular" featuring such stars as Crosby, Maurice Chevalier, and Frank Sinatra in brief cameo appearances, has been all but removed from both television and motion-picture showings.

On the set of Bob Hope's Alias Jesse James

OTHER MISCELLANEOUS FILM APPEARANCES

1. **THE ADVENTURES OF ICHABOD AND MR. TOAD** (Walt Disney–RKO, 1949) Bing Crosby and Basil Rathbone narrated this Walt Disney cartoon feature.

2. **THE SOUND OF LAUGHTER** (Union Films, 1963; directed by John O'Shaughnessy). A largely unsuccessful film featuring movie clips of forgotten comedies of the thirties, this little curiosity was narrated by Ed Wynn and contained some extremely rare early shots of both Crosby and Hope.

3. **CINERAMA'S RUSSIAN ADVENTURE** (United Roadshow Presentations, Inc., 1966; directed by Roman Karmen, Boris Dolin, Leonid Kristy, Oleg Lebedev, Vasily Kafanian, and Solomon Kogan). Bing Crosby provided the narration for this Cinerama-eye view of Russia.

Dr. Cook's Garden
An Afterword

It is ironic that Bing Crosby's last screen role to date should be the most atypical characterization of his career. Although it was never distributed for theatrical release, this 1971 television movie must be included because it contains one of the performer's most memorable acting portrayals.

As the film's title character, Doctor Cook, Crosby appears as a mild-mannered New England physician, visited by a younger doctor named Jimmy (Frank Converse), who has admired Cook ever since childhood and has now decided to return home after a long absence. Much to his horror, Doctor Jim soon learns that Doctor Cook has been practicing medical homicide on the sick and elderly of the village to keep the town as perfect and disease-free as possible.

Once Doctor Cook learns that young Jim has found out about his scheme, the old man feeds his young assistant a poisoned ham sandwich during a picnic. The young fellow goes through a series of horrible convulsions, but at the last moment, quick thinking enables the young doctor to trick Cook into administering an antidote.

Back at Cook's office, the old man tells Jimmy that he hates killing and that he resorts to murder only out of pity for the sick. Jimmy admits to Cook that he tricked Cook into giving him an antidote, and this sends the old man into a psychotic rage, during which he attempts to kill Jim with a garden hoe.

During the struggle, the old fellow's heart gives out and he pitches to the ground, gasping desperately for air. Jim runs inside to get the old man's nitroglycerin tablets but finds himself unable—or perhaps unwilling—to save the doctor's life. "Help me, Jimmy. Please!" says Doctor Cook.

Jim looks at him with a tinge of pity and says, "I think I am, Doc."

With a knowing smile, Cook then tells him, "You see how it begins."

An enormously effective horror film produced for television by ABC and Paramount, *Dr. Cook's Garden* is of particular interest because it is the first time the performer ever portrayed a villain. There can be no doubt that Doctor Cook was a deranged individual, but Crosby's performance in the role is far above most other portrayals of screen psychos. His Doctor Cook is neither a raving madman nor a ruthless killer. Instead, Crosby skillfully molds his Doctor Cook into the kind of personable elderly gentleman whom anyone might welcome as an ideal neighborhood physician.

Crosby manages to convey beautifully the image of a kind and considerate doctor whose mental sickness is kept quietly under lock and key until the scene in which he attempts to poison the young doctor. In this scene, one of the most tense and dramatic sequences ever to grace a teleplay, all Doctor Cook's prior calmness dissolves into desperate psychosis as Frank Converse simulates the convulsions of a poison victim with unnerving realism. It is a superbly played interlude, proving that movies for TV can be effective and that Bing Crosby's talent as a dramatic actor has sharpened with time.

With his family and Fred Astaire in the CBS-TV special, A Couple of Song and Dance Men

The Recent Crosby/An Epilogue

In spite of his illness a few years ago, Bing Crosby seems more determined than ever to stay active professionally, both in the United States and abroad. He has awed his fans and the press by recently undertaking a strenuous series of show-business assignments, including the partial narration of a major Hollywood nostalgia film, two beautifully produced and performed record albums, several television appearances, and a three-hour stage show, *Bing Crosby on Broadway,* which opened at New York's Uris Theatre on December 7, 1976, and ran for a limited two-week engagement. Bing's Broadway performance received a series of glowing reviews in major newspapers and magazines, but it should be pointed out that this stage appearance was, more than anything else, the superb culmination of a comeback effort that began the moment the performer recovered from his illness.

1974 could go down in show-business history as the year Bing Crosby decided to end his semiretirement and step back into the limelight. At that time, Crosby agreed to act as one of the star-narrators of MGM's tribute to its own musical films. *That's Entertainment.* In addition, 1974–75 also saw the completion of a hit record album, "Bing Crosby—That's What Life Is All About," as well as the production of an hour-long television special, "Bing Crosby and Fred Astaire: A Couple of Song-and-Dance Men." In the latter, Bing was reunited with his co-star from *Holiday Inn* and *Blue Skies* for an hour's worth of songs and nostalgia, culminating in a nicely staged re-creation of the duet from *Blue Skies* in which Bing and Fred again told what it's really like to be a couple of song-and-dance men. As an interesting sidelight, the restaging of "A Couple of Song-and-Dance Men" on the TV special was neatly interspersed with clips from the 1946 film's original production number, giving audiences an opportunity to compare Crosby's and Astaire's mellow and nostalgic 1975 interpretation of the song

As he appeared in That's Entertainment, *1974*

With wife Kathryn at the Crosby home in Hillsborough, California being interviewed by Mike Douglas for the November 21, 1975, edition of "The Mike Douglas Show."

Bing on Broadway

with their bouncy, fast-paced approach of thirty years earlier. The television special's impressive roster of songs were later put on a record album ("Bing Crosby and Fred Astaire: A Couple of Song-and-Dance Men," United Artists Records, 1975), which still enjoys a handsome sale.

In addition to his special with Astaire (not to mention his perennial Christmas specials, which continue to delight audiences every holiday season), Crosby put in a unique appearance on daytime television's "Mike Douglas Show" in November 1975. The show was especially delightful in that Mike Douglas actually interviewed Bing and his wife Kathryn at the couple's home in Hillsborough, California. Appropriately, the show ended with Crosby casually strolling around the enormous garden surrounding his house, singing his latest hit, "That's What Life Is All About," while practicing his golf swing.

Bing Crosby on Broadway, presented as a musical-light-comedy revue and featuring nearly fifty songs, also starred Bing's family (wife Kathryn, and children Harry, Mary Frances, and Nathaniel), along with Rosemary Clooney, the Joe Bushkin Quartet, and British comedian Ted Rogers. The highlight was Crosby's rendition of "White Christmas," which was especially appropriate because the production enjoyed its two-week run during the Christmas season.

Although thirty-odd years have passed since Crosby first introduced the song in *Holiday Inn*, his 1976 rendition cannot help but remind the audience that this is the same performer who filled 1942 movie screens with an almost idyllic vision of the Christmas season.

In perhaps *Holiday Inn*'s most memorable scene, Bing soulfully croons "White Christmas" to Marjorie Reynolds amid the homey innocence and comfort of the Holiday Inn's sitting room, the beauty of which is accented by a fire blazing away in the fireplace. At the conclusion of the song, director Mark Sandrich slowly fades the scene to black while gradually intensifying the background fire, so that the audience's last image of the scene is a stunning shot of Crosby and Reynolds smiling at each other, their faces illuminated by the shimmering firelight.

This scene left its audiences with a warm feeling about Christmas, and Crosby arouses this very same feeling every time he sings "White Christmas" today. It is a marvelous testimony to his magic as a performer.